WAITING FOR THE MORNING

WAITING FOR THE MORNING

▼

A Mother and Daughter's Journey through Alzheimer's Disease

Brenda Parris Sibley

Writers Club Press
San Jose New York Lincoln Shanghai

Waiting for the Morning
A Mother and Daughter's Journey through Alzheimer's Disease

All Rights Reserved © 2001 by Brenda Parris Sibley

Writers Club Press
an imprint of iUniverse.com, Inc.

For information address:
iUniverse.com, Inc.
5220 S 16th, Ste. 200
Lincoln, NE 68512
www.iuniverse.com

ISBN: 0-595-18782-X

Printed in the United States of America

In memory of my mother, Jessie Lee Parris, 1916-1996
I'll always love you, Mama.

And in your memory I walk every year in the
Alzheimer's Association Memory Walk
in Huntsville, Alabama

CONTENTS

▼

List of Illustrations ix

Acknowledgements xi

Introduction xv

Chapter 1 Coming Home 1

Chapter 2 Mama's Little Girl 12

Chapter 3 Home for Christmas 27

Chapter 4 Winter Thoughts 42

Chapter 5 Long Winter Nights 48

Chapter 6 Seeing Things 56

Photo Album 69

Chapter 7 Birthday Blues 76

Chapter 8 Finally Spring 91

Chapter 9 Solemn Summer 108

Chapter 10 Summer's End 118

Chapter 11 Falling Down 129

Chapter 12 Nearing the End 139

Chapter 13 The Last Christmas 149

Chapter 14 Sitting Alone 164

Chapter 15 Through the Tears 174

Epilogue 189
About the Author 205
Bibliography 207

LIST OF ILLUSTRATIONS

▼

Mother in her favorite tee-shirt, 1994–Introduction xv

Mother at back door of house–Chapter 1 3

Mother in her chair, smiling–Chapter 2 14

Mother standing by Christmas tree–Chapter 3 29

Mother getting bundled up
by Myrtle for walk outside, 1994–Chapter 4 44

Mother sitting in her chair, 1995–Chapter 5 50

Mother leaning over in her chair, 1994–Chapter 6 58

Photo Album section: 69

Mother as little girl with doll, about 1924................................69

Three photos of Mother and Father as newlyweds in 1934 70-72

Mother and Father in 1959..73

Mother and Father in 1976..74

Mother with first grandchild, author's niece, Dawn, about 1968...........75

Mother sitting in her chair with new dress on, 1995—Chapter 7 78

Mother sitting in her bench with new dress on, 1995–Chapter 8 93

Mother sitting leaned over in chair, 1994–Chapter 9 110

Mother on 4th of July holding puppy, 1995–Chapter 10 120

Mother with author's sister, Myrtle, brother-in-law,
     Simeon, and niece, Donna, 1994–Chapter 11 131
Mother touching flowers, 1995–Chapter 12 141
Mother on bench in garden, 1995–Chapter 13................................151
Mother sitting in her chair, 1995–Chapter 14 166
Mother and Father in 1970s at lake–with poem *Daddy*...................173
Mother at back door, 1994–Chapter 15 176
Mother touching flowers–with poem *Precious Times* 179
Mother sitting in her chair–with poem *Sights and Sounds* 181
Mother in the city (Chattanooga, TN) about
     1940–with poem *Song of Alzheimer's* 184
Mother with niece's doll on soft throw rug at Christmas,
     about 1974–with poem *What I Wish* 186
Mother and puppy on 4th of
     July 1995–with poem *Sing to Me, Mama*....................................188
Mother sitting on bench in garden,
     1995–with Dorothy Womack's poem *Most of All*.....................192
Mother on bench under peach trees–with poem *I'll Remember* 195
Mother walking outside with Myrtle,
     1994–with poems *Singing Trees* and *Out that Door* 197
Mother as little girl holding doll,
     about 1924–with poem *Little Girl Again* 200
"Quilt" constructed of "patchwork pieces"
     of my mother's dresses—with poem *Mama's Quilts* 201
Mother with Myrtle, Simeon, and Donna,
     1994–with poem *Heroes* 203

ACKNOWLEDGEMENTS

▼

How do I begin to thank all the people who helped me during my time with my mother and after? And those who gave me the little push needed, the encouragement to get this book into print? I am filled with gratitude toward those who helped me make it through, to those who comforted me afterwards, and to all who have helped me in sharing my mother's story.

My family was there for me through it all—my sister Myrtle, especially, and my brothers William and Bob. Their husbands and wives were there by their sides and offering me support as well. I'm so grateful for the help of my family through my caregiving experience and afterward.

My Alzheimer's support group, Caregivers, a ministry of the Parker Memorial Baptist Church and Interfaith Ministries in Anniston Alabama, was a pillar of strength and water in a desert. They provided information, coping skills, and most important of all—they let me know I was not alone. The group's leader, Mrs. Betty McGinnis, encouraged me to keep my journal. Later, she also encouraged me to publish it, and she printed several of my poems and excerpts from my journal in the *Caregiver's Newsletter*.

The Cleburne County Home Health was always there when I needed them. Aides came three times a week to help my mother get a bath, and nurses came every two weeks and whenever I needed them, to check my mother over and to discuss problems with me. They also provided me with a break from the routine and a smiling face to cheer my mother and me. Nurses Becky and Carmen, and all the aides—I wish I could remember all your names now, but I remember the faces, and most of all I remember and deeply appreciate your kindness.

I want to thank my friends—so many of them—who wrote encouraging letters to me, who comforted me on the phone upon the nursing home decision, who emailed me often during my difficult days following my mother's death. Among these are Karen Sue and Sonia from Florida State University, Lucy, Doreen, and Jessie who I had known from living in south Florida, and Lois who has been a good friend since I met her at work in Radford, Virginia.

Almost immediately after the placing of my mother in the nursing home, a surprise came into my life. I met Richard, and I have teased him that if he were more angelic I would think he was an angel sent to take care of me after all that I'd been through. I cried on his shoulders often in the months after my mother's death, and he encouraged me to get all the feelings out, to go through the journal, and whether published or not, to express my emotions so that healing could begin. He has also been my number one fan and my toughest critic as I began sharing my mother's story through my home page on the Internet.

There are so many people to thank for helping me to share this story through my page on the Internet. First of all, though, I must thank my ISP, HiWAAY Information Services of Huntsville, Alabama. They gave my page one of its first and most cherished awards. I received HiWAAY's Best Home Page of the Year for 1996—just a month after it was uploaded when it was just a few poems, pictures, and a few links to Alzheimer's resources.

I also wish to thank Zarcrom.com, who later, when I moved out of HiWAAY's area, awarded me with 50 mgs of free space for my site. Their generosity and their excellent service are deeply appreciated.

I must thank the *Alzheimer's List* at Washington University at St. Louis for their Web site and for the mailing list/discussion group where I told my story and received comfort and support. I also want to thank *CANDID* in England for their Web site and the Candid-Dementia list and chat room. Thanks also goes to Rivendell's Griefnet for its Web site and mailing list and to the wonderful people I met there and on the Usenet group alt.support.grief. There are so many people I've met on the Web that I feel I need to thank, but I hesitate, knowing that I will leave out many that I should mention. Thanks to Bob Hoffmann for his wonderful Web site and for asking me to share my story through his column in *Caregiving Newsletter*, and to Denise Brown, the editor, for publishing it in the September 1997 issue. Thanks to Suky and the Florida Support Network for their great Web site and for sharing my "Song of Alzheimer's" in their Mother's Day 1997 issue of their newsletter. Thanks to so many others who have asked to use my poems and excerpts from my journal—I am always happy to share in any way I can.

Thanks so much to the Alzheimer's Association for being there for us all. The Alabama chapters responded to my desperate calls early in my caregiving experience, sent me information, and got me connected with my support group. I am fortunate to have lived in the Huntsville area, home of the North Alabama Chapter and to meet its former Executive Director, Kim Holbrook, and also for living briefly in Troy where I met Kay Jones, Director of the Southeast Alabama Chapter in Dothan, who was so helpful to me and sent me a copy of *The 36-Hour Day* (Nancy L. Mace and Peter V. Rabins. 3rd ed. Baltimore: Johns Hopkins Univ., 1999) when I began taking care of my mother.

Again, I return to my Web friends, and there are some extra special ones I cannot leave out. I have already mentioned Bob Hoffmann. His was the first personal homepage by a caregiver that I found on the Internet. Another was by Marilyn Schaeffer. Then Susan Grossman—and her highly reviewed *Alzwell* site, where I have added a memorial to my mother and have written on the "Anger Wall" several times. And more recently, Marsha Pennington with her amazing *Alzheimer's Outreach* site. Still a little later came people who have became very close friends: Dorothy Womack and Brenda Race, wonderful poets, writers and Web authors who have become my dearest friends; Nancy Walker, a nurse and talented Web author with Alzheimer's as her cause; and Kate Murphy, who had a wonderful caregiving site before mine came into existence and who became an editor for *Caregiving Today*. The sites of all these talented caring people, and many others are linked on my page at http://www.zarcrom.com/users/yeartorem/homepages.html. To the wonderful people linked there and to all the Alzheimer's and caregiving-related and grief-related sites, I owe a huge debt of gratitude.

Thank you to all who have presented my page with awards, both great and small, and for all who have reviewed it. Thanks to the Japanese newspaper that did a story about my page and Bob Hoffmann's; to USA Today for making it a Hot Site in November 1996; to WAAY-TV in Huntsville, AL for making it a Web Site of the Day in December 1996; to The Net magazine for reviewing my site in January 1997; and to ZD-TV's "Internet Tonight" for featuring my site on their show in January 1999. I could go on and on thanking people for awards and reviews, and for every Web page where mine is linked, but all of you know how much I appreciate it, because you know the importance of this story. I thank you so very much for helping me share it with others.

Thank you to Anna Necklaus, a student at Calhoun Community College where I work, for helping me decide on the title of this book, choosing it from my poem by the same title. Thank you also to Anna for encouraging me to complete this project, saying she wasn't going to stop bugging me until it was published.

Last of all, but certainly not least, I wish to thank the people at iUniverse.com, especially Valerie Haas-Redmond, without whom this book would not have made it into print. This is a wonderful time of opportunities for anyone who wants to be published, and I highly recommend iUniverse.com. It's a great place for those of you who, like me, have a story to tell but haven't yet been successful with traditional publishing; or those who of you who wish your work to be in print much faster and made available through the Internet as well.

INTRODUCTION

▼

My Mother's Story

How long had our mother had Alzheimer's? My sister and I have asked ourselves that a thousand times since the diagnosis of dementia in 1993. We know it must have been at least fifteen, maybe even twenty years. Her memory had been going for a long time, but she's just getting older, we had thought. Her math skills went first, and she had been letting my sister take care of her checkbook and bills for several years. She had been repeating things she said for a long time, and getting things someone else had told her all mixed up when she tried to repeat them. Living in another state, I looked forward to her letters, but it got harder to read them (She said she didn't have my dad to spell for her anymore. He died in 1985), and eventually they stopped. She continued to call me. But after I moved to Tallahassee to go to Florida State, she no longer called me. When I called her, she would say that she had tried and tried, but she couldn't get my number.

That was four months before her stroke. My sister, who lived next door to my mother, went to visit as usual, but in the middle of the day, she couldn't get my mother awake to come to the door. Finally, she did get there, but my sister thought my mother was never going to get the door open to let her in. Finally she did, but my mother had come to the door without a top on.

My mother was hospitalized for a week. Then she went home, and my sister went through hiring several sitters before she found one that could handle taking care of my mother. Though even at that time she had not been diagnosed and it was thought that there might be a chance for her to recover from the stroke, she was very aggressive and combative. My sister ended up staying with her every night. She hired a sitter to take care of her in the daytime, but the first summer, she took care of her day and night.

I had been at grad school for only a few months when my mother had her stroke. I said then that I would come home, but my sister insisted that I stay at school, saying that she could handle it. I didn't know till later that she was getting physically sick from the stress of taking care of my mother, especially that summer that she did it alone. She lost twenty pounds and began showing signs of age.

Meanwhile, I was trying to finish graduate school and work full-time, but I could not concentrate, because I felt I needed to be home taking care of my mother. I was the logical one—the only one who was divorced, with no husband or children to look after. My family didn't say this, but I felt it myself. Overloaded with course work, I ended up taking an incomplete in one class, having to stay around a year to make it up, and barely struggling through my classes. Finally I left, needing only twelve hours to finish my degree, but knowing I could not wait that long. My mother needed me, and I had to go home.

In ways, my sister had gone through the worst of taking care of my mother, when she was in a more alert stage, constantly having catastrophic reactions and being aggressively combative. After I came home, she was getting into a calmer stage, except at night. The night wandering didn't begin until I came home. And that was good, because my sister would never have been able to work the next day after being up all night with my mother.

I took care of my mother from the end of August 1994 until the end of December 1995. This is the story of that time and the months that followed after my mother was placed in the nursing home. It comes from the journal I kept during that time, the poetry I wrote then and since, and treasured photographs of my mother and family.

Come share my mother's Alzheimer's journey, and my journey as a caregiver. Learn from my mistakes, know that you are not alone, and most of all, cherish the time you have left with your loved one.

CHAPTER I

▼

COMING HOME

Mama

Walking through the house
that doesn't feel like home;
You've forgotten it,
as well as all your children.
One day you woke up, and
those memories were gone.
You walk the floors and worry,
wishing for cattle and land,
for food, for cash crops.
You just can't understand how
it is today—why we don't need all that.
Your mind is still in the years
of the Great Depression.
So you walk and worry.
I try to explain, tell you
there's nothing to worry about.
I cook, and I tell you when it's
time to eat, and I give you your pills.
I clean the house.
I'm here for you, Mama.
We've got all we need;
We've got each other.
Please don't die, Mama;
You're all I've got.

Tuesday, August 23, 1994

I guess I've always been a dreamer, always had such high hopes, always thought I could save the world. With every year I've lived, with every dream that has died, I've come to realize I'm just one more human, struggling to survive each day, and I cannot change the world.

Yet, I thought it would be different this time. I'm my mother's baby, her little girl, who she loved so much. Surely I'm the one person who could make it all better for her. All I had to do was to quit school and come home to live with her, and she would be all better.

I couldn't have done otherwise, after hearing her wish for that so much, and seeing her cry so hard as I left at the end of each visit.

So I came. My announcement on Saturday along with the flowers brought the desired effect. She cried and laughed and grinned from ear to ear all day. But it wasn't long until that wore off. Sometimes I think she doesn't know me at all.

My dreams of making my mother all better show how little I knew about Alzheimer's, I guess. But I had to do this. And it is an adventure. I never know what will happen each night, how many times she will get up thinking it's morning, or the things she will say in the middle of the night. I'm off now, to another adventure.

Saturday, August 27, 1994

I have been here for a week now, and I am over my initial shock at my mother not knowing me, and I'm over my "What have I done?" phase of earlier in the week. This feels good. This is good. For a change, I'm giving a little of myself, and I like it.

My mother and I are getting along just fine. There are times when things don't go terribly well, but I'm learning what works and what doesn't. I've even been rewarded a couple of times in the past two days with her saying, "I love you, and I'm glad you came to stay with me."

That's worth it all, all the waking up at night, all the trouble getting pills down, and trying to get her to eat when she doesn't want to, and all the endless questions, same questions over and over about people from the past and about other people she thinks are living in this house.

Yes, I'm glad I came home—very glad. I hope I can help make the rest of my mother's life just a little more pleasant.

Sunday, September 18, 1994

I have been with my mother a full month now. Only in the last two days (and nights) have I seen what my sister had told me about—the bad part of some sort of cycle my mother goes through that seems to happen about the same time each month (the full moon, maybe?), when my sister describes our mother as actually being mean.

I slept no more than three hours last night. Tonight I slept only an hour, but I don't dare go to sleep now, at 2:00 a.m., even though my mother has finally fallen asleep, not in bed, but in her chair in the living room. I don't dare try to get her back to bed. When I did that last night, it took over an hour of walking through the house and even outside to get her calmed down. She was looking for "that girl" who would "take me home and show me where to sleep." Every time we walked through the bedroom, I showed her the bed and asked her if she wanted to lie down. But I couldn't convince her that this was her home and that was her bed. Finally she went to sleep in her chair between 1:00 a.m. and 2:00 a.m., and then she got up at 4:00 a.m. and went to sleep in her bed until 6:00 a.m. I got two of my three hours of sleep on the couch from 2:00 a.m. to 4:00 a.m.; then I couldn't go back to sleep.

Tonight she got up looking for "the baby". She had already expressed some anger towards me when I helped her go to the bathroom. Then she had a dream and woke up talking about something that was dangerous for the baby, that would poison it. She wandered around the house for a while, and then just before she fell asleep in her chair, she told me "You watch the baby; Don't let anything happen to it." I worry that one of these nights she will wake up looking for "the baby" and not finding it, think I've done something to harm it. All I can do is sit up and watch her as she sleeps, hoping that when she wakes she will have forgotten, for tonight, her obsession with "the baby."

I'm so tired. But I have to stay awake. Most of the time when I do fall asleep, my mother wakes and is angry because I'm not doing something she thinks I should be doing.

I don't know how long I can do this. But I'm still glad I came. I will do my best; I will try to take good care of my mother for as long as I can.

Monday, September 19, 1994

Yesterday was a wonderful day, even though it didn't get off to a pleasant start. I didn't get any more sleep until 7:30 p.m. last night when my mother went to bed, and I too, fell into bed exhausted, without bothering to take a shower.

After sitting up much of the night, at 3:00 a.m. I thought she was going back to bed, but when we got there, she wouldn't go; She said she couldn't, and she just sat there. So we went back to the living room, and she sat in her chair again.

At 4:30 a.m. she seemed wide awake, so I thought I would go ahead and start breakfast, because most mornings she was up by this time anyway, even if she did spend more of the night in bed. But by the time I got breakfast ready, she had fallen asleep again. I waited until she woke up. Then I asked her to come eat breakfast. She said no, that she wasn't hungry.

I tried again at 6:00 a.m., but she still said she wasn't hungry. I asked her about getting a shower and getting dressed, because we always went to my sister's (next door) for Sunday dinner. She said no, she wasn't getting a shower, she wasn't getting dressed, and she wasn't going anywhere all day.

I waited an hour or so before trying again to get her to eat breakfast. Finally around 7:30 a.m., when I asked her if she could eat a little breakfast, she said, "I guess so." She ate about three-fourths of her breakfast before saying she couldn't eat anymore (usually she eats half or less).

After breakfast, I asked her again about getting a shower, and she again said no. I did the dishes and then sat by her for a while, and maybe an hour later, I asked her again. She still refused the bath, but she agreed to put on a dress. When I asked her about going to my sister's, the answer was still no. Each time, the way she responded and the mumbled words made me wonder if she really knew what I was asking.

She went out to sit in the swing on the front porch (a favorite place) for a while. Then she came back and asked me what it was we needed to do, why did I say we needed to go to town. I told her that we didn't need to go to town, but we'd been invited by my sister, her other daughter, for Sunday dinner, just like always. She said she didn't feel like being around so many people. (There's only my sister and her husband).

She walked through the house and out to the back yard, and I followed her. We were going in the direction of my sister's house, and she asked "Is too early to go to Myrtle Lee's?" I told her no, that I just needed to run back and lock the door. I did and quickly called my sister (I had called her a few minutes earlier to tell her we weren't coming.)

It was a wonderful day! My mother ate well, and she didn't get restless till mid-afternoon. Though she enjoys being at my sister's once we get there, she often wants to leave as soon as we've eaten, if not before. But it's good for her, I think, and it gives me a break, the only break I get except for one Saturday a month shopping and when my sister visits each week-day afternoon for about an hour when she gets home from work.

I've had some rough times already, and I know there will be more, but days like this one turned out to be make it all worthwhile.

Friday, September 30, 1994

It's now 4:30 a.m., and I've been up with my mother since midnight. Actually, we've been up and down since midnight—this is the third time that she's come to sit in her chair in the living room. This time she's having one of what my sister calls her "dying spells." It appears to be indigestion usually, but this time there seems to be some neck and ear pain, and she's fallen asleep now in her chair using a heating pad.

Every time the Home Health nurse comes, my mother seems to be in good shape—good blood pressure and temperature. The nurse always hears a lot of gas in my mother's stomach. One day this week I called the nurse because my mother was having chest pains and thought she was dying. The nurse came, and everything was fine. She got her to take the Alka-Seltzer® that Mama wouldn't take for me, and then she started feeling great, attributing it to the nurse who came and saved her life.

Until this night, she's been sleeping better at night. I don't want to give her more Thoridazine® unless I have to. Sometimes more seems to make her more hyper instead of relaxed.

Sunday, October 9, 1994

Things have been going along very smoothly the past couple of weeks, except for an occasional "dying spell", as my mother has a bout with indigestion. Lately there have been some nights of getting up at midnight or 1:00 a.m. to sit up the rest of the night, but no "catastrophic reactions" (the term the books on Alzheimer's use) of any major proportion until tonight. I really brought on a big one of those today. And, as the books say and as support group people have told me, it is indeed the caregiver who usually brings them on.

This time it was not my voice or attitude or anything I was aware of until tonight. This morning, after I had helped my mother get a shower and get her dress on, I sprayed a little perfume on her dress as I was spraying some on me. I had been noticing an odor, and I just wanted her to smell nice when we went to my sister's for Sunday dinner.

Apparently she was allergic to the perfume and suffered all day with burning and a rash, and she wasted no time in having a catastrophic reaction as soon as we got home, telling me she had blisters all over from the "powder" I had "thrown" on her this morning, and that I was treating her "like a dog."

I tried to explain, to tell her I didn't know she would be allergic to it, gave her a soapy cloth so she could wash herself off, helped her change into a gown, and the more I did, the more her angry words and actions continued. She didn't hit me, but she drew back her hand as if she were going to—this she has done a couple of times before.

She finally calmed down after I helped her into a gown and put on a "Little House on the Prairie" (NBC, 1975-1982) video for her to watch. Though I know I'm not supposed to show emotion, I did let a few tears run down my face as I was sitting there with her. I hoped she wouldn't see, but apparently she did. She started apologizing, and going on and on saying she was sorry.

She is sleeping now, but I can't. I don't know what else might happen tonight. I'm not doing so well with this. I need to be completely non-emotional, to speak always in a soft voice, and to stop trying to explain, because explaining doesn't work and only seems to confuse her more. I have so much to learn about Alzheimer's. I need to know everything I can find out now before she gets worse.

Thursday, October 13, 1994

I decided today that I won't be my mother's daughter anymore. I'll be whoever it is she thinks I am. And in that, I think I may have discovered how to get along with her. It's also the only way for me to get myself past the feelings of rejection. Somehow I think she senses those feelings but she doesn't understand them. So both of us will be better off if I can just be her hired girl, or one of her hired girls, as it sometimes seems she thinks I am.

I have one success story already. I haven't been able to get my mother to eat more than three bites of her meals for the past three days. About an hour ago I got her to eat a whole bowl of oatmeal (at my second attempt today of trying to get her to eat breakfast).

I've noticed the Home Health aides can usually persuade her to let them give her a bath, and I've noticed how they talk to her "…honey, sweetheart, Miss Jessie…", so I took the food to her and did that, and she ate it all.

I think, too, that I've learned the secret of smaller, simpler meals. A larger breakfast, with more different foods, even if there's just a little of each, looks like too much to her, or is confusing to her, and she just won't eat it. I've found out she won't eat much in a regular size bowl either, but if I put it in the smallest bowl I can find, she will usually eat it all.

Another thing—I will stay away from her if it's not meal time or snack time or pill time, unless I can get her to take a walk outside or go to the porch. She seems to want to be left alone as much as possible. She's told me so at times.

I'm feeling good about this new me. I think this is what some of the books call "distancing yourself." They say for some people it takes longer than others, but it has to come at some point for a person to be able to continue to take care of a family member who has Alzheimer's.

Monday, October 16, 1994

Does Alzheimer's affect the brain at all like schizophrenia or a multiple personality disorder? If not, why does my mother seem like several different people? She changes personalities every time she wakes up from a nap. Sometimes she's a playful little girl. Sometimes she's an old woman about to take her last breath. Sometimes she is loving. Sometimes she is cruel, almost violent. Some days she likes certain foods, and other days she hates those foods. Is it just a matter of memories, of waking up with memories from different stages of her past, and of her dreams as well? Sometimes it really seems like there's different people there.

Everything seems so backwards, too. Sometimes she stays up all-night and then sleeps in her chair all day. She even makes comments about it being night sometimes when it's in the middle of the day. Sometimes when I tell her to put her dentures in, she tries to take them out. She often does the opposite of what I tell her she needs to do.

And she's slipping more everyday. She can't find the bedroom or bathroom. She can't turn the water on and off to wash her hands.

I've been here two months now. I wonder how much longer we'll be able to keep on going, just handling the day to day things. I don't want it to end. In spite of it all, I love being here. But can I handle it if it gets worse, or I should say, when it gets worse?

Thursday, October 27, 1994

Every time my mother has one of these "dying spells" (indigestion?), I get so scared. She wants all her kids around her, wants things settled, and says she's going this time. I think "Please, no, I'm not through painting the kitchen, and I still have to put down the new kitchen floor." She hardly notices, but she would be so thrilled if she were still herself. I've got so much to pay her back for; I need a year with her, at least. I want to see her eyes when she sees the Christmas tree, and when she sees the flowers next Spring.

I know it's just indigestion, and I know she'll be better after I get her to take something for it, but for a while each time she really does look like she's at death's door. She was okay for the rest of the day after she got better from her indigestion today, but she slept a lot in her chair.

Saturday, October 29, 1994

There is some kind of cycle here. Also there seems to be some kinds of relationship between the different factors. During the period she's in now, my mother doesn't want to stay in the bed, but she does sleep more soundly, even in her chair, so much so that she is incontinent.

I'm still puzzled as to why she wants to sleep in her chair. Why does it seem a torture for her to sleep in the bed and so pleasant to sleep sitting up in her chair? Just one more of the many things that is backwards, turned around, opposite of what it should be.

I'm fascinated by this illness. There's no way I would give up now and allow her to be put in a nursing home—not yet. I have to observe, to write down, to discover the cycle, the relationships. I have to understand Alzheimer's, for her sake and for mine.

CHAPTER 2

▼

MAMA'S LITTLE GIRL

It's Me

Mama, it's me,
I'm your youngest daughter.
Can't you see that; don't you know
who it is that loves you so?
You ask the others; they tell
you, too, that I'm your baby,
I'm your Sue.
Why have you forgotten me?
I'm right beside you; can't you see?
Mama, please look into my eyes,
please tell me you love me
and that you're glad I've come.

Wednesday, November 2, 1994

I try not to be upset when my mother doesn't eat, but it makes me feel like I'm not taking good care of her. There are times when she will, but the times when she won't are getting more frequent. Yesterday I fixed a big pot of soup. She saw me doing it, even asked if she could help. Then when it came time to eat, she refused. It wasn't that she didn't like that kind of soup. I made it for her several weeks ago, and she seemed to love it then.

So at times like these, I get out the Ensure®, and I'm thankful for that. But there was that nice warm pot of soup that I thought was so good on a cold night, and she didn't want any of it. My trying to get her to eat and her refusal gets us both in a bad mood, which starts other things happening.

We made it through the night alright, surprisingly, but then strange things started happening this morning. She got up talking about my ex-husband and me, except that she doesn't know it's me here with her, and to her the person she was talking about is still in Florida. When I tried to tell her who I am, and that I was the one he was married to, that got her all mixed up. She thought I was "the one" who took him away from me. This is so confusing, and so painful for me. And I hope this is not one thought she will remember, because it would only add to her anger towards me on the nights when she is so confused. At least "the baby" hasn't been in her confused nighttime conversation lately, so maybe this too will be forgotten.

Saturday, November 5, 1994

I'm seeing a cycle more clearly now and am more able to predict when certain things will happen, though the dates are not exact, and still sometimes things will happen when I least expect them. But there is a phase when she is incontinent, followed by a time when she is up all night, followed by no appetite, and then the dreaded phase when she is most likely to have catastrophic reactions. This last phase consists of at least two severe outbursts from one to three days apart, and most likely they will happen in the middle of the night. She had been through the other three, and that last phase is coming up soon, so I watch and wait. At night when she is up, I read a book about Alzheimer's in search of some help and comfort, and I hope, how I hope, she doesn't remember during this time her confused thought of the other day, that I am the girl who took my ex-husband away from me!

Monday, November 7, 1994

Every time I think I've got things figured out, my mother (or I should say Alzheimer's) proves me wrong. She has been eating well. She's had another period of incontinence, and then last night there were a couple of catastrophic reactions, but they didn't seem quite as bad as usual.

The first one was around 11:00 p.m. She thought she was going to have a baby, and she wanted me to get someone to help. She couldn't seem to understand when I told her she wasn't going to have a baby now and that there wasn't anything to worry about. I offered to help her go to the bathroom if she needed to, but she wouldn't. She just sat on the side of her bed like she was waiting for someone. I lay back down on my bed and watched her as she sat there. Finally she asked me if anyone was coming to help her have her baby. I told her (maybe it was the wrong thing to do, but sometimes going along with it all doesn't work either) that she wasn't going to have a baby, that she was seventy-nine years old and that she couldn't have a baby. I helped her go to the bathroom, and then she went back to bed and slept till 4:00 a.m.

Then at 4:00 a.m. she was out of the bed and trying to get her dress on. I tried to help her, but after getting just one sleeve in she fought and pushed me away, saying she didn't need any help and she didn't like anyone to help her get dressed. She ended up in the living room with just one arm in the sleeve of her dress, her gown back on over it, one shoe on, and trying to put her wrap (which we throw over her legs) on as if it were pants. I tried to help, to explain that was just a little blanket to keep her legs warm, and that she couldn't wear it like pants. After her struggling for fifteen minutes, I again offered help, and she had given up. I got her gown off, her dress on right, and put the wrap over her legs, explaining again that was what it was for, finally making her understand its purpose, I think.

And so I began another day, more tired than I was the night before.

Tuesday, November 8, 1994

After a bad start yesterday, something special happened in the afternoon. Or at least it seemed that way for a few minutes. I spent most of the afternoon sitting by my mother as we talked. She was clearer than she'd been in a long time. It started off with her hugging me and crying and saying she had just realized who I am. For much of the afternoon it sounded like she really did.

Then she started asking me about relatives I hardly knew, as if I were part of that family I had not seen in a long time and knew very little about—nieces, nephews, and cousins from my dad's family.

She moved on to talking about my ex-husband, and then about me as if I was not here, and again, I knew she could not accept who I am. She even mentioned our talk of last week when she thought I was the one who took my ex-husband away from me, and she said "When that girl was here, it was all I could do to stand it—listening to her talk." I tried to tell her again that was me and that I was only trying to explain who I was. It was like it just confused her so much that she just quit talking then.

It's so confusing, and scary when she gets so mixed up like that, and when she remembers something like our conversation last week. Again and again I learn, trying to explain something to someone with Alzheimer's does no good. It only makes everything worse by confusing them even more. But at least there are those times when there's a glimpse of the person she used to be, even sometimes, a brief moment when she seems to recognize me.

Sunday, November 13, 1994

We were off to a bad start this morning. My mother said she had an upset stomach, caused by something she ate yesterday. She kept talking about that at breakfast and wouldn't eat much of it, because she said it was the same thing that made her sick yesterday. Telling her it wasn't the same thing, of course, did no good, but rather agitated her.

Surprisingly, the rest of the day went fine, my mother ate well, and it was a good Sunday at my sister's house.

Monday, November 14, 1994

We were up at 2:45 a.m. this morning. My mother no longer seems to understand me when I tell her that it is still night, that the house is cold, and that we would be warmer in bed. The house is freezing. I guess I'm going to have to start leaving these gas heaters on all night, because I never know when my mother will get up. I'm glad I got her a good warm robe the other day, and that I was successful in getting it on her last night. Now I just need one myself. I finally got warm and could no longer stay awake—fell asleep on the couch about 4:30 a.m. Within 10 minutes, my mother was awake.

My mother was asleep again by the time I got breakfast ready. I warmed it up about forty-five minutes later when she woke up, but she wouldn't eat it. She took one bite and told me it tasted awful. All I've got down her today was a little Ensure® and a banana, and she frowned when she was having those, like I was making her eat and drink something terrible-tasting. She's definitely in her no-appetite stage again.

Wednesday, November 16, 1994

It's so different this month—not at all as predictable as I thought. There have been no major catastrophic reactions and seemingly no attacks of indigestion until today. Lately my mother is becoming more like a baby who can't tell me what is wrong. When I see her looking like she's in terrible pain or distress, I ask, and often she tells me nothing hurts. Then she tells me she's having a hard time getting her breath, and I know it's probably indigestion.

There is no way of predicting anything, because everything seems to happen differently each time. I never know what she will want to eat today, which movie she would like to see—if any—before bedtime, whether she will stay in bed tonight, and when the next catastrophic reaction will be and what will bring it on.

I'm afraid that sometimes I bring them on. I worry about her not eating, and I try to get her to eat more, and she refuses and gets upset. Often it is either that or the medicine, which she hates taking and sometimes has a hard time swallowing.

The book I'm reading now says that unconditional love works with Alzheimer's, "When you can really love your mother exactly as she is, she can reemerge and be who she used to be for a while." (Davidson, Frena

Gray. *The Alzheimer's Sourcebook for Caregivers*. Los Angeles: Lowell House 1993.) I've seen it happen, sometimes when we watch movies together, sipping hot chocolate or tea, and when we walk around outside looking at the flowers together. We do have some good times. I just wish they lasted longer before the bad times came again.

Saturday, November 19, 1994

It is 1:00 a.m. We have been up since midnight. Most nights, my mother thinks it's time to get up at least a couple of hours before it really is. Every time she gets up to use the bathroom she asks, "What time is it?" or "Is it time to get up?" or "Is anybody up yet?" Sometimes after I say "no", she says, "I thought I heard someone up in there." I used to try to say that there's no one here but us, but I've found out it works better to just say "No, no one is up yet."

But some nights, like tonight, telling her it's not time to get up just won't work. She's up and out of the bedroom almost before I can say anything. It's like she can't hear, or can't understand, anything I say. Usually she's looking for something or someone, or she's going to "wait up for" someone. Sometimes she has a headache, a neck ache, an earache. Sometimes there's no explanation, she just wants up and out of that bed and into her chair, her "other bed"—yes, that's what she calls it sometimes. She often says she's "going to bed" when she wants to sit in her chair, or that she's going to "lie down" in it. (It's a big old rocker, not a recliner.)

Tonight she was hunting something; I couldn't figure out what. After she finally sat down in her chair, she said she would stay there till I could "fix a bottle for her." It took me a few minutes, but I finally found out she had a headache and wanted something for it.

I was suprised that tonight has turned out to be a night of being up all night. My mother was up much later than usual. My sister and brother-in-law were here with her, and I was late getting back from shopping—7:00 p.m. I have a hard time getting my mother to stay up till 7:00 p.m.; Usually she wants to go to bed by 6:00 p.m. or 6:30 p.m. So I've seen tonight that keeping her up later doesn't necessarily mean she will sleep longer.

It's 2:00 a.m. now. A few minutes ago my mother was awake and wandering through the house, saying something about "those men." She seemed to be expecting someone and worrying because they weren't here. On nights like this, telling her it's the middle of the night and that no one is coming does no good. Her dreams, hallucinations, and delusions are so real to her.

She slept again in her chair, then she awoke again and walked through the house a couple more times, and now at 3:30 a.m. she is asleep again. The last time she was awake, she mentioned "Waiting for U.S."—her deceased husband, my father—I couldn't tell her that he is dead.

Again, she woke and wandered, and now at 4:30 a.m., she is asleep again. It's strange, when she's in bed she usually gets up every hour, sometimes more often, to go to the bathroom. This night, she's only gone to the bathroom once since midnight.

I have read all night as I have sat up with my mother. I've just finished *The Alzheimer's Sourcebook for Caregivers* (Los Angeles: Lowell House, 1993) by Frena Gray-Davidson. It's the best one I've read other than *The 36-Hour Day* (Nancy L. Mace and Peter V. Rabins. 3rd ed. Johns Hopkins Univ., 1999).

I got the impression from this book that the increased sleeping in the daytime may be one of the symptoms of the more advanced stages of Alzheimer's that my mother is getting into. It sounds like things like not being able to eat, or walk, or being incontinent aren't necessarily going to happen.

Another thing the book points out is that nursing home care doesn't necessarily have to be, even in the final stages. Many Alzheimer's patients die in the first few weeks in a nursing home. They just never recover from the shock of that kind of change. And if they don't die, many never recover from a loss of function that they experience at that time.

I saw a temporary loss of function in my mother not long after I came home. Just that much change seemed to make her much more confused at night. She didn't begin getting up and staying up at night or her nighttime wandering until I came home. Though she is better in ways now, the getting up at night is only increasing.

She must be protected as much as possible from drastic changes that might upset her. I still wonder, and worry, did my divorce almost two years ago bring on her stroke and a rapid advance in the Alzheimer's that we had not realized she had? Her stroke was just two days after my divorce was finalized.

Tuesday, November 22, 1994

I think that we have passed the bad time for this month, without any big problems except around the 6th, and those weren't really so bad, though they might have been if I hadn't backed off and left her alone for a while. Sometimes it seems that's the only thing that will work.

This month there have been very few times when my mother had no appetite, she's had very little incontinence, and only a few nights of being up all night with no really bad catastrophic reactions.

However, the indigestion, or what appears to be indigestion, has been getting worse, and if we don't catch it early enough each time, it gets so bad that she thinks she's dying.

We've had some good times out walking when the weather is nice. We've had some unusually warm and sunny days, and that has helped, but in the next few days winter will be beginning, and I dread all the days when she will have to stay in the house and can't get out. We went through some of that a few weeks ago when it was raining a lot, and she was really depressed during that time.

We never sleep till daylight. I can expect her to get up between 4:00 a.m. and 5:00 a.m. each morning if not sooner, but we go to bed early each night—I usually do almost as early as she does, so it doesn't bother me much.

I look forward to having the holidays give her something different and more exciting, but I also dread the way thinking of such things sometimes depresses her. She talks a lot about her parents, and I know the holidays may make her miss them, and my dad when she remembers him, even more.

Friday, November 25, 1994

We had a problem yesterday morning at a time of the month when I didn't expect one, but I guess it could be all the excitement of Thanksgiving that did it. My mother thought she was dying, and I insisted she take something for indigestion, she refused, and I still insisted because I wanted her to feel well enough to enjoy Thanksgiving. She hit me then, and I gave up. The hitting doesn't bother me so far—it doesn't hurt at all. She didn't do it hard, and I don't think she wants to hurt anyone anyway. She just wants to be left alone.

I did that, going to another room with a book to read. In a few minutes she came looking for me, crying and apologizing, saying she was afraid I left. I knew then that she would cooperate with taking a shower and getting dressed to go to Thanksgiving dinner at my sister's. All went well there. Mama had all her kids around her, even though she probably didn't know any of us, and she seemed content.

It's 2:00 a.m. now. Mama just got up and headed for her chair, with no explanations given. I was able to get her robe on her and a throw over her legs. Luckily, I put a nice new warm gown on her at bedtime. She does seem to pick some of the coldest nights to get up. I think it's about twenty degrees tonight. I had left the heater on in the living room and began turning the others on around midnight, so it's warm enough now, but not as warm as it would be in bed.

It's 5:00 a.m. now, and my mother and I have been talking since about 3:00 a.m. when she woke up from sleeping in her chair. She had a hundred questions, and I think she repeated each about twenty times. It was like she couldn't understand a thing I said, or that she forgot it as soon as I said it.

She had a dream, I think. At 3:00 a.m. she asked me "When did your daddy die" and "Who was your daddy?" It was like it didn't sink in, no matter how many times I told her, that he had died nine years ago, that he was her husband, and that she was my mother. Finally, I think, I got her to understand that was a long time ago, but she still was convinced that someone had just died. She started asking about "that girl that died", and I think she was meaning me, because she sometimes seems to think there are at least two of us. She's always asking, "What happened to that other girl that came with you?" I think she thought one "the girls" left yesterday when I left her alone and went to another room to read. After me answering her about twenty times, telling her no one had died, no one had left, it was just a dream—finally I got her to understand, or perhaps by then she had forgotten what she had been asking.

Saturday, November 26, 1994

We are up about thirty minutes later than yesterday morning—it's 2:30 a.m. (We were up the rest of the night yesterday). I'm so tired. I shouldn't be, because we've been in bed eight hours. But it seems like we were up every thirty minutes for my mother to go to the bathroom. The last time we got up, she asked "Can I live in that chair in there?"

We had a good day yesterday. I read to her, and she even recognized a few words herself and could read them, like "the" and "a" in the titles of the stories in the large print *Guideposts* (Carmel, NY) my sister had subscribed to for her. The rest of the day we watched Christmas movies, in between naps. I had to have a couple of naps, too. Eight hours of sleep or not, getting up around 2:00 a.m. makes me tired the next day. I'm wondering if I'll be able to do it this time, even with a two-liter of diet cola with caffeine at my side. I'm afraid to fall asleep, but I just can't keep my eyes open much longer.

It's 7:45 a.m. now. I managed to stay awake till 4:30 a.m. this morning, and then I just couldn't stay awake any longer, so I fell asleep on the couch. And sure enough, my mother was up within ten minutes asking me what was I doing lying down there.

So I went to fix breakfast. I had got dressed an hour earlier when she was awake and said she was hungry, but I didn't fix breakfast because she fell asleep in her chair again. When I got breakfast ready at 6:00 a.m. she said she wasn't hungry, and she ate only a couple of bites.

A funny thing happened. When she was up and out of her chair a little after 5:00 a.m., she was laughing and said I had the same disease and was worse off than her, because I was talking about chickens when we didn't have any. It seemed everything I was saying about fixing breakfast and her eating, she thought I was talking about chickens. In fact, she had been talking about them herself at 3:30 a.m. (She and my dad had raised chickens on the farm for about thirty years), and I had tried to explain to her that there were no chickens raised here anymore. When I told her that again when she brought up chickens, that the old chicken houses were in too bad shape to be used, her laughter seemed to turn into fear, then confusion, then lack of trust for me, and thus later, no eating breakfast. When will I learn to quit trying to explain things to her?

Sunday November 27, 1994

It's now almost 3:00 a.m., and this is the third night in a row that we've been up, though my mother did stay in bed until 2:30 a.m. She almost had a catastrophic reaction when I tried to help her put on her robe. I just let her walk away, and then she saw that she did need it, and she let me help her.

Now at 3:45 a.m., I sit watching her, observing. She's been sitting in her chair for the past hour, hardly opened her eyes at all since she's been there, though she is moving around, sometimes rocking, shuffling her feet, propping her head on her hands.

The nights of being up are increasing each month. She hasn't been incontinent as much. And the catastrophic reactions haven't seemed so bad. Lately when she gets up at night, she just sits in her chair, sleeping off and on, with no more wandering, searching for "the baby" or wanting to "go home".

I'm writing again at 8:30 a.m. At about 4:00 a.m., my mother started asking me questions. She seemed to have dreamed that my brother Bob was coming to get her to take her home with him, and that was why she was sitting up waiting. She said he'd sent her a message. I had the hardest time getting her to understand it was just a dream. Then she started talking about wanting to "go home." Finally I realized what she was saying was that she wanted to go back to bed. She said she didn't know how she had got there and she wanted to go back where she belonged.

Monday, November 28, 1994

Last night wasn't bad. My mother didn't get up till 4:00 a.m., and then as soon as she got to her chair, she wanted to go back to bed, saying that no one else was up.

It's a rainy day, and days like this seem to make things worse. My mother has had no appetite today. She didn't eat much at breakfast, and she ate even less at lunch.

My mother was teasing me this morning about messing up her house with the plants I'm growing. Soon the teasing changed into her walking through the house and saying everything was a mess. So I began frantically cleaning house (even though I do keep it pretty clean). She went to sleep, and then woke up not speaking to me or eating.

The "bath lady"—a Home Health aide came then, and after she left, my mother was so mad at her. She said she "cut" her ear with the comb when she was combing her hair. I think it upset her that the aide was talking to me, too. She doesn't like it when the aides and I carry on a conversation. I can see it by the way she looks, and how that look grows the longer we talk.

Tuesday, November 29, 1994

It is 7:45 a.m. and all is well. My mother slept all night, ate her breakfast and let me help her take a bath because one of my sister-in-laws was coming. My mother got her first Christmas present of the year during that visit—a good warm quilted fleece pants and top outfit. She appreciated the gift, and afterwards she kept saying she had to get her something, even though she didn't know who she was. She said once that she was the lady who used to stay with her.

Wednesday, November 30, 1994

I was trying to help my mother get her pants on this morning, and she got mad at me, said she was tired of me telling her what to do. I told her I was just trying to take care of her, and she said no, that I was just bossing everything she did. So I left her in the bathroom to get dressed herself.

She came out after somehow managing to get her pants on herself this time. She went to the front porch, letting a blast of cold air in the door. She turned back and saw me, and she started telling me, proudly, how she had just told the other girl off. I told her it was me (unwisely). She asked what I'd got mad at her about, and why couldn't I get along with her. She said I'd better let her just leave and find some place else to live, that she could find a little place to live and take care of herself.

It's so strange what losing one's memory does to a person. She was the one who was angry, and yet she thought it was me. If it were like this all the time, I don't know if I could do this much longer. But there are the other times, the good times.

CHAPTER 3

▼

HOME FOR CHRISTMAS

Christmas Past

Oh the days of Christmas past.
how I wish them here again—
sitting in Daddy's lap,
holding Mama's hand.
Through school days,
and church Christmas plays,
off to college and back again.
There always was family,
always was home,
always was Christmas back then.

Thursday, December 1, 1994

We were up at 4:30 a.m. after my mother questioning for an hour "Do we have to stay in this place? Is anybody going to come and let us out of here?" It seems she got cold and couldn't sleep. She doesn't like me to have the heater on in the bedroom at night. She's afraid I'm going to "burn the house down." I did have it on from about midnight till 3:00 a.m., but then I saw her getting restless, and I turned it off, fearing she would be upset with me for having it on.

So now she's sitting bent over in her chair, looking like she's about to fall out of it as she sleeps. I dread morning after her having slept like that; I dread the confusion that it may bring on.

Saturday, December 3, 1994

My mother stayed in bed for only four hours tonight—in bed at 7:00 p.m. and up at 11:00 p.m. She had complained of a leg ache at bedtime, but when she got up at 11:00 p.m. and again when I asked a few minutes ago, she said she wasn't hurting. Her reason for getting up was that she just couldn't stay there, just couldn't sleep in bed. She's been asleep in her chair most of the time so far except for when she got up to go to the bathroom a few minutes ago.

I don't mind much being up tonight. It gives me time to do things I was afraid I wouldn't have time to do tomorrow. I'm doing a Christmas tree decorating dinner, having the family here this time for Sunday dinner. I had been afraid I wouldn't have time to do everything, with getting my mother and myself ready in the morning and handling any confusion or even catastrophic reactions she may have. So this way I get a head start. I've put the ham in the oven, made a congealed salad that is now chilling in the refrigerator. I may make the pear salad in a few minutes, maybe the tossed salad, too. Maybe I can get it all done, except that I don't think I could stand smelling beans and peas cooking until after breakfast, and the potatoes will be better done later, too. Any noise I make doesn't seem to bother my mother. Sometimes she seems to sleep better in her chair if there's a little noise going on in the kitchen.

I was just about too excited to sleep anyway—couldn't go to sleep myself till around 9:00 p.m. I had just went to sleep, it seemed, when my mother got up, so I really don't mind tonight. I'll keep running on the caffeine in my diet cola till our Sunday get-together is over, and then I'll take it easy on Monday.

Sunday, December 4, 1994

It's 1:45 a.m. now, and the dinner is coming along, the ham is baking and two salads are in the refrigerator. My mother slept through all of it, until just now when I sat down.

She got up and mumbled about cooking something, and I don't think she understood anything I said when I asked her if she needed to go to the bathroom or if she needed something. She got up, said she was looking for something (to cook?). I turned on the overhead light. She said she couldn't find it, and she would just have to cook the others.

She fumbled with her robe, which had been wrapped around her shoulders, and with her leg wraps, attempting to fold them and lay them aside. Then she sat back down and went to sleep again.

I'm glad this happened tonight instead of a few nights ago when it was colder. I didn't have the heaters on when she woke up, but now it is nice and warm in here. That's good because she wouldn't let me put her robe on her, so I just put it around her shoulders. Now she's just sitting there in her gown with neither her robe nor her wrap. I'm glad it's one of her warmest gowns. I asked when she was awake if she wanted her wrap over her legs. She replied "No, leave it alone." I think that would have been said again with an exclamation mark if I had persisted.

I guess my mother was having a dream about cooking (perhaps because she knew I was cooking?) and was acting it out. I'm glad she didn't go to the kitchen and actually try to cook. It's better to go along with it. Telling her it's just a dream doesn't do any good. Sometimes she will nod her head when I say that, and then she will say something like "Well, he said he was going to pick me up", obviously referring to someone in her dream.

Saturday, December 10, 1994

I've just noticed that our nights of being up seem to occur mostly on weekends, and probably most of the catastrophic reactions do too. I wonder, could they be a reaction to change? Perhaps so simple a change as my going off shopping once a month on Saturday? And having Sunday dinner at my sister's?

My sister was off work yesterday, so I went shopping on a Friday this time. And we were up at 3:00 a.m. this morning. That's not too bad, though. The night before it was at 11:00 p.m.

I just looked back over my calendar, and yes, most of the catastrophic reactions have been on weekends, or on holidays, or any time there was change—me going shopping, the two of us going to my sister's, people coming here.

I've been with my mother four months now. No matter what we go through, I don't regret coming home.

We looked at old photo albums today, and my mother identified all the old ones from fifty to sixty years ago and even some more recent ones. She identified all of her children (except me). She identified the pictures of my ex-husband as the man that was married to "Sue" (she always called me by my middle name), but she can't see that I am "Sue". She says I don't look like her. But she thinks I'm someone who knew her.

This is what hurts most. Not her behavior, not staying up all night, not the catastrophic reactions, but the fact that she doesn't know, or won't accept, who I am—this is what hurts most.

Sunday, December 11, 1994

We were up at 1:00 a.m. My mother had asked earlier if anyone was up. The next time she got up she didn't ask, just reached for her clothes. I talked her out of putting them on, because there's always the chance she might go back to bed if she doesn't get dressed. We almost had a reaction when I tried to help her put her robe on. I didn't realize that she had to go to the bathroom immediately.

It's so much better now than it was in my first month here. Even though she's getting up more often, there isn't the wandering through the house looking for "home" or "the baby" like there was then. We're doing alright.

Monday, December 12, 1994

Yesterday at my sister's wasn't too bad, except for some communication problems. My mother had already begun the day asking me questions. It's so hard knowing just how to answer, when she often doesn't understand what I'm saying anyway. Then at my sister's, an old friend came to see my mother, and that brought up childhood memories. My mother got a little upset with my sister because she couldn't remember what she was talking about. She thought she should be able to remember her childhood, because at the time, she was thinking she was her sister, not her daughter (That's what she thinks much of the time).

Other than that, the day went fine, even though my mother showed no interest in the Christmas tree that was being put up. After the tree decorating, I napped on the couch for a little while. It seems that's the only time I get real rest—on Sunday's at my sister's. I can sleep knowing they are looking out for Mama and that I don't have to be listening for her even in my sleep.

Surprisingly, my mother slept all night last night. But this morning wasn't a good one. She was worried about us using the gas heaters, and she said I was going to burn the house down. I tried to explain that it was freezing outside and that those were the only heaters we had to keep us warm. Then her worrying shifted to "the children", and I told her that her children were all right, all grown up and in their own homes. We went through an hour of talking about things like this before she was calm enough that I could leave her long enough to fix breakfast.

After eating breakfast, she announced that this was her "last day", that she "wasn't going to do this job anymore", that she was "going to let the man know when he came", that she was "too old to take care of all you kids." (She's always talking about "the man", and none of us can figure that one out.) I told her she didn't have anything to worry about; everything was fine, that I was here taking care of her right here in her own home. Then she said she didn't like this house, that it wasn't any good, and that she was leaving.

She's sleeping in her chair now, after getting up agitated a few more times. I don't know what's brought on all this—maybe something she dreamed last night? It's so scary because dreams are so real to her.

Tuesday, December 13, 1994

We had a bad time early this morning. My mother had been trying to get up all night since about 10:00 p.m. Each time, I would tell her it was still the middle of the night, and she would go back to bed. That didn't work at 4:00 a.m. She was up and wanting her clothes on because someone was "bringing the berries." After I helped her get dressed, I said I would go cook breakfast. She snapped back at me that there was nothing to cook because "they" were not here with it yet. I told her I'd be in the kitchen, and she said she was going to tell Myrtle (my sister, who she usually thinks is her sister—unfortunately they had the same name) what I said and I would have to leave.

All through breakfast she was convinced I had said something terrible, but she said that she would forget it and forgive me and she wouldn't tell Myrtle this time. I could stay, but I'd better not do it again, she said. She added, "I know you lied to me."

I think my problem is telling the truth instead of lying. I just haven't learned how to play along with her the right way. And it's so hard to understand what she's talking about at times.

One other thing she said this morning—that this was her house and I wasn't getting it. I'm afraid I may have brought that on by trying to fix up the house a little in my first month or so here. I have stopped that now, and probably should have sooner.

A couple of weeks ago when I went shopping, my mother told my sister that she had given me all her money to buy groceries and she was afraid I would run off with it and not come back. I never take much from her, but she had given me a little extra, saying that she wanted me to buy Christmas presents for all her kids.

After this morning's incident when she said she would forgive me and forget what I'd said, I asked her "What did I say?", and she said "I don't know. I didn't hear it. One of the others told me."

She thinks there are several of us here, not just me with her. Often when we get ready to leave my sister's, she will ask, "Where's that other girl? Is she coming with us?" We ask her who, and she says "That other girl that came with us."

Sunday, December 18, 1994

Sleeping was back to normal the rest of the week. Then I went shopping, and that night we were up at midnight (I know—too much shopping—but it's almost Christmas!). Not long after getting to her chair, my mother began looking confused. By 12:30 a.m. she told me she didn't know how she got there and that she wanted to go back to bed.

Then an hour later, she's up again, saying she just wants to sit in her chair. When we were up at midnight she asked me "Who are you?"

I had a feeling this would be one of those nights. My mother wanted to take her throw that we keep over her legs to bed with her, because she said the cover in the bed was no good. Then she wanted to move one of her pillows halfway down on the other side of the bed to for her head. I told her there was another pillow on that side of the bed, and she told me I was awful. As she lay down she said she didn't know how she could get to sleep on such an awful bed.

We were up the rest of the night after 1:30 a.m. My mother did a lot of talking in her sleep, as she sat in her chair. I couldn't understand much of what she said, but once she said something about "a picture". The day didn't start out well. My mother refused her Sunday bath, and she said she wasn't going to my sister's for Sunday dinner. She refused a morning snack, saying she couldn't swallow, and was holding her chest and throat, saying it hurt. I knew it was probably indigestion, so I got her something for it, but she refused, saying she just wanted to die. I told her I loved her and wanted to help her feel better, and she said "You don't do anything but poke stuff down me that the doctor says I'm not supposed to have." I told her I was just trying to make her comfortable and to stop the pain whenever she hurt. She finally let me give her something, and then she fell asleep. When she woke up and walked through the house, admiring the sunshine through the window, I asked her if she wanted to go out and walk in the sunshine, thinking maybe I could still get her to go to my sister's. But she said, no, that her legs hurt. I will call my sister and tell her. I'll just fix something for the two of us to eat here today. It's not long till Christmas, and I'll have to insist then, but we can skip today.

Tuesday, December 20, 1994

My mother was up at 1:00 a.m. looking for "U.S."—my dad. She doesn't do this often, but I dread the times when she does. I don't know what to tell her. Sometimes it's like just now finding out if I tell her he'd dead. It's the same way when she asks about her parents. I never know what to say.

She kept walking through the house looking for him for about a half-hour. Then she went back to bed, but she kept getting up, sitting on the side of the bed, asking about him three more times before she ever lay down and went to sleep—about 2:00 a.m. Then she was up again at 3:00 a.m., saying she was going to sit in her chair. And that's where she slept the rest of the night, as I sat up and watched her.

Sunday, December 25, 1994

It's Christmas morning. My mother has no interest in opening the presents under the tree. She's refusing to go to my sister's for Christmas dinner. She hardly touched the special Christmas breakfast I fixed for her. She says she's going to die today. She refused to take anything for what must be indigestion. She's still in her nightgown. We can skip the bath if we have to, but I've got to get her into some clothes when she wakes up from the nap she's taking now. I won't mention going to my sister's. I'll just see if I can get her to take a walk the way we did last Sunday. If not, I guess we'll just have sandwiches here for Christmas Day.

At least we had yesterday—a Christmas Eve drop-in party with finger foods. I did that because one of my brothers has a big family by marriage and can't come on Christmas Day. It all went well when everyone was dropping in one at a time, but last night everyone showed up all at once and were here together for about an hour. I saw that bothered, confused look on my mother's face then. That may be why we're having this problem today. But it was the same way a month ago, on Thanksgiving Day.

Now at 7:30 a.m., my mother has been to the bathroom a couple of times, and a few minutes ago she told me where she wanted to be buried. I could hear her stomach rumbling, and I asked her to take something for it. This time she didn't refuse. We might have a good Christmas Day after all.

And it was, a good day. It's 8:00 p.m. now. At about 9:00 a.m. this morning, my mother let me help her with a bath and getting dressed. We went to my sister's and had a good day. All went well until a few minutes ago.

About a half-hour after we got home tonight my mother became angry when I was helping her get ready for bed. She told me she didn't need me anymore and wanted me to leave so she could find someone else to stay with her because I was always saying "mean" things to her. I just went ahead with helping her get ready for bed, and then I let her sit in her chair. Sometimes I think it would be better if I said nothing to her.

I think at times she hears something completely different from what I say. She honestly believes I've been saying mean things to her.

It was a good Christmas, in spite of this. It was good being with all the family, and having my two nieces home. My mother was showered with gifts, and she has plenty of warm comfortable clothes now. So let the cold winter come, and even nights up like this. We are ready.

Monday, December 26, 1994

We slept all night last night! At about 9:00 p.m., Mama said she wanted to talk to me. She tried telling me about what happened with that "other girl", my "sister", and that she didn't really want her to leave, that she needed her. I assured her that I knew that, told her I was the "other girl", that I was here staying with her full-time. Then she decided to go back to bed, and she slept till our usual getting-up time, 4:30 a.m., without even asking about getting up any earlier.

She's slept off and on in her chair most of the morning since breakfast, of which she took only a few bites. Once when she seemed wide-awake, we watched part of a Christmas video—still trying to finish the ones we were loaned for the holidays.

One of my nieces is still here, one granddaughter still to visit my mother sometime this afternoon before she leaves tomorrow. But there will be no more crowds. I'm having the family for New Year's, but I'm not going to fix so much as I did Christmas Eve, and I'm not going to mention it till it's here.

Wednesday, December 28, 1994

It's 2:00 a.m., and we've been up for about fifteen minutes. My mother has been trying to get up since 11:00 p.m. or earlier. I haven't slept much of the night because each time she woke me up, I haven't been able to get back to sleep until, it seems, just before she got up again.

Yesterday was a good day, after the usual confused and sleepy morning hours and no appetite at breakfast. The rest of the day she was asking for food, and for a change, eating everything in sight! The weather was nice, and we took three walks outside.

I look forward to seeing the flowers coming up outside in the next few months. The walks will be fewer because the weather will be cold, but when we do get out, it will be wonderful to see my mother's delight when the crocus, hyacinth, and daffodils begin blooming. She got warm jackets, gloves, and socks, as well as warm pantsuits for Christmas, so we can bundle up and go see it all happening soon. Maybe it will make the times we spend inside better, too.

My mother just went to the bathroom, and when she came back she said she was going to get everybody together and tell them she couldn't go on this way, she wanted to be taken somewhere, that she wasn't like this before I came, and something had to change.

It must have been a dream. But one good thing is whenever something like this happens, she will soon forget it. When the sun comes out brightly today, hopefully she will be in a good mood, and we will go outside and enjoy the pansies which are still blooming their hearts out.

She seemed content a few minutes ago when I said, "OK, I'm sorry, I've failed.", and I assured her that I would tell my sister that she wanted me to leave. Tonight she's happy with the idea of me leaving. Tomorrow she may hug me and tell me I'm sweet. Tomorrow night she may hold my hand as usual while we're watching TV. In another week we may go through some bad nights again. But she always forgets, and she becomes sweet and loving again.

There was a pleasant surprise on the day after Christmas when my niece visited. My mother seemed to recognize me for a little while. She asked my sister about "that girl who claims she's mine", and then my sister pointed to me and asked who I was, and she said "Sue". (My mother always called me by my middle name.) I guess she thought I was here just for Christmas, but she hasn't asked if I'm still here or if I left.

Her not knowing me bothers me more than anything does. If she just knew me, that would make it all so much better. She wouldn't tell me to leave if she knew I was her Sue, her baby daughter. She wouldn't be depressed so often if she knew that I, her Sue, had done what she had asked me to do—actually come home to stay. If only she knew.

Thursday, December 29, 1994

We were up for an hour at 11:00 p.m. last night, after having a not-so-good day yesterday. My mother was talking in her sleep last night and said something about babies, then she got up, said she had a headache, refused to take anything for it. She told me she did this lots of nights (as if I didn't know) and she went to her chair, where she fell asleep. She got up an hour later and told me she was going to bed, and she actually stayed there till 5:00 a.m. this morning!

Yesterday morning we were watching a movie, and all of the sudden she got up out of her chair and said she wanted that Christmas tree down and that mess cleaned up and out of her house. So I started taking the tree down, but she didn't want those boxes in the floor, so instead of carefully packing my ornaments (some very expensive and fragile), I just piled them in the boxes and took them upstairs as quickly as I could. While I was doing that, she was complaining about me going to break her ornaments. Later she talked to me about "that other girl" and what she had done that morning.

Friday, December 30, 1994

We were up at midnight for my mother to go sit in her chair and sleep. A little later she awoke and began acting out a dream. She asked me for a knife. I went to the kitchen and brought her a spoon, hoping that would do. Then she was looking for the okra she was going to cut up. I convinced her (I think) that it was a dream, and she told me I should get a job somewhere else. Then she sat back down in her chair and fell asleep again. At 3:00 a.m. she wanted to go back to bed. But as soon as I'd fallen asleep, she was back up again for the rest of the night. At 5:00 a.m., I just couldn't stay awake any longer, so I lay down on the couch, but five minutes later, she was up again.

Today I did something I rarely do—napped in the daytime. My mother was sleeping in her chair, so I took a nap on the couch beside her. I was asleep at 3:00 p.m. when we had relatives come for a visit, and I know I acted strangely because I was so deeply asleep that I could hardly get awake to answer the door. In fact, my mother got there and opened it before I could. The only other time I've done this, a Home Health nurse caught me and I don't think she liked it very much. She said "You know, they can get away if you're not watching them." Maybe it would be better if I go ahead and try to sleep at night when I'm up with her, as long as she's sleeping in her chair.

Saturday, December 31, 1994

I did get a couple more hours of sleep early this morning, but it didn't work out so well in the end. When I woke up, my mother was staring at me. She said, "Get back over there! You took this job, so get back over there and take care of the babies!" I just sat down. Then in a little while I told her I was sorry I had fallen asleep, but now it was time for me to fix breakfast, and I was going to get dressed and do that. She didn't say a word, but she kept staring at me. Then at breakfast, she ate wonderfully—every bite for the first time in a long time. She asked me about the children, and when I told her that hers were all grown up and she would see them all today, she seemed satisfied with that answer.

Today is New Year's Eve. Instead of a party like Christmas Eve, I'm just making a pot of soup that will go with sandwiches. There's hot apple cider, hot chocolate, and hot teas for afterwards, to go along with leftover Christmas goodies. And tomorrow I'll do fifteen-bean soup (including black-eyed peas, of course), my sister will do the traditional southern collard greens, and my brother-in-law will do cornbread. No big deal this time—just a drop in Saturday night and an ordinary Sunday dinner. Just relaxing, warming-up with some hot food and drinks, and enjoying being with family. Hopefully all will go well.

CHAPTER 4

▼

WINTER THOUGHTS

Come Spring

Things will be better come Spring I know
when all the world is abloom.
Our walks will be long and frequent then
when the garden comes alive and the birds sing a tune.
The garden spot I'm planning there will be
your favorite place, just wait and see.
No more days of sitting in the house;
You and I will be out all the time.
You can walk through the garden or sit on the bench,
and I'll work in the soil, the pleasure's mine.
With flowers abloom all around you,
you'll feel better then.
We will picnic in the garden
on fresh vegetables we've grown;
It will all be more pleasant
than anything you've known.
Yes, though now in the dead of winter,
will be well come Spring
when the vegetables grow in the garden
and the birds gather round the flowers to sing

Sunday, January 1, 1995

We were up at 10:30 p.m. last night. My mother said "You need to fix it (the bed) because I'm not getting back in it" as she went straight to her chair, not letting me put her robe on her (which is ok tonight, but it won't be a few nights from now when the temperature drops into the teens).

It was so funny how my mother woke up from sleeping in her chair about a half-hour before midnight. I turned on the TV, thinking it might be ok, and that we might as well see the ball drop at Time Square since we were up. My mother enjoyed that. Afterwards, I asked if she wanted to go back to bed. She said it didn't matter to her. I told her it kind of mattered to me because I needed to sleep since I was going to be cooking a New Year's dinner. So we went back to bed, but just for an hour.

Something happened this morning that changed our New Year's Day plans. Apparently I used up all the water in the well this morning. After being up at 1:00 a.m., we went back to bed at 2:30 a.m., and then at 4:30 a.m., my mother woke up, finding me asleep, and told me that I should be washing clothes, that we girls weren't working together, helping each other. I did have some washing to catch up on, so I did it.

So since I'd used up all the water in the well (I'm learning, it doesn't take more than a couple of loads of clothes to do it), we decided to have our New Year's get-together at my sisters. Everything went pretty well till we got home. My sister and brother-in-law came with us for a few minutes to make sure the well was ok and to look up some genealogical information that my niece wanted. My brother-in-law was in the living room with my mother, watching a comedy show on TV. As soon as they were gone, my mother went to the bathroom and took off her pants, and I saw why she had been looking disturbed. She had needed to go but wouldn't because my brother-in-law was there. She was upset with me as I helped her get into a gown and again when I was giving pills—she said I'd already given them to her (She'd just had a vitamin at supper). She didn't want to watch TV as we usually do a little before bedtime. She looked sleepy, so I asked if she was ready to go to bed, and she said she wasn't, that she didn't think she could, and that I should just lock up the house.

She had an incident of incontinence just before I woke up this morning, too. Or maybe it was just not being able to figure out how to get to the bathroom. She had made it there, passing up the bedside potty, put the lid down, and then proceeded to use it. I'm glad I took out the carpet in that bathroom and replaced it with tiles.

Monday, January 2, 1995

I got my mother to go to bed at 9:30 p.m. last night, and I gave her a second Thoridazine® at that time. Then we were up an hour later. I think we might have been at midnight, too, if I hadn't been successful in convincing her it was still time to be asleep. Maybe that second Thoridazine® helped. She's to have two at bedtime, but I've been giving her only one, because if I give them to her at the same time, she will be incontinent. Maybe one at supper and another at bedtime might work better. I think two may be too much at times, and at other times one isn't enough.

An incident of incontinence this morning makes me think this must be a time when two is too much. Also she's been really sleepy and confused this morning and didn't eat breakfast. Maybe the second Thoridazine® was too much. It helped me get some sleep for her to sleep more, but I don't like the way she is today. She's been so sleepy, it's like she's hardly waking up all day long.

Tuesday, January 3, 1995

It's 1:00 a.m. and we've been up for about half an hour. My mother would have gotten up an hour earlier, but I told her the house was too cold and that I needed to warm it up, which was true. She had said she had a headache, so I gave her an aspirin. When she got up just now, I had the house warm enough now, but she wasn't happy with me for not letting her up earlier, and she also said "You didn't ever bring me that aspirin, and my head is killing me!"

After at least an hour of being awake and restless, my mother has now fallen asleep in her chair. She kept saying her feet were cold, so I changed her from socks to the fuzzy warm house shoes she got for Christmas. She complained that the new stool my brother-in-law made for her didn't work because it made her feet cold when she used it. I tried to explain that it was to rest her feet on, not to warm them, and that we'd have to wrap her feet up good to get them warm.

Friday, January 6, 1995

There are times my mother needs more Thoridazine® at night, and I just have to figure out when those times are. Lately I've been giving her more, the amount the directions on the bottle say to give. She has been sleeping all night till nearly daylight, and I feel so much better being able to do the same. I'm not sure I like the daytime affect though.

CHAPTER 5

▼

LONG WINTER NIGHTS

Waiting for the Morning

I sit awake with you
in the scary midnight darkness,
telling you everything is okay,
calming you down after a dream,
holding your hand as you wander,
searching through the house
for remains of your former life.
I sit as you sleep in your chair,
when you won't go back to bed,
knowing you will wake in terror,
afraid of a dream, afraid of not knowing,
afraid of everything.
And sometimes you won't hear,
my words will be as meaningless
as the ones you sometimes say.
And perhaps you will reach out,
sometimes searching, sometimes striking;
I'm here for you, whatever you need;
I'll even be your punching bag.
But I can't fix things for you;
I can't bring your memories back.
They are gone, just like the house
and people you search for.
All I can do is sit and wait
with you for the approaching dawn
when things will look a little better
illuminated by the light of day.

Wednesday, February 1, 1995

My mother had very little appetite yesterday morning and the night before, but she regained it by lunchtime yesterday. She started telling me no one had been giving her anything to eat. And she was worried, saying she didn't have the money to pay for anything to eat. She held up a couple of paper towels and ask if that would pay for something for her to eat.

She had seemed pretty clear yesterday afternoon at 2:30 p.m. when we took a walk around the house, but by 3:30 p.m. when my sister arrived for a visit, my mother was just sitting and staring from her chair.

We were up this morning at 3:00 a.m. I have kept a record of the nights we've been up much of the night. They increased every month until January, which was the same as December.

I have just put away all the knives. I didn't think this would be necessary before, but this morning just before 5:00 a.m. I was so scared that she would find them. She was looking for one, she said "to peel the potatoes". She started rummaging through the drawers for one, and I gave her a spoon. Then she went all over the house in search of "the potatoes." She got angry with me because I couldn't help her find them, but she finally admitted there were no potatoes, and she sat down and fell asleep as I fixed breakfast.

Thursday, February 2, 1995

Yesterday we had a really good afternoon. We had the warmest weather in weeks. My mother wanted to walk outside. And she did—three times! She was out of breath each time when she got back, and she sat down to take a nap as soon as she got back. But just getting out made her so excited—so different—once she even wanted to run! Come spring—maybe things will be different most of the time.

Maybe then she will even want to stay awake in the daytime and be active enough that she will sleep more at night. Maybe.

Saturday, February 4, 1995

We've had a very strange night tonight. My mother was fine today. I was even thinking it was so wonderful things were getting so much better. But then as evening came, things began to get strange. She didn't want supper, but I told her she needed to eat at least a little so she could take her pills. Then she wanted to take her pills all at once, not spread out as we do them before bedtime, because she said she just had to get some sleep. After supper, I tried putting a movie in the VCR, but she didn't want to watch it. I managed to get her to take her pills, and then she was in the bed by 6:30 p.m.

Just before she went to bed we talked a little about what was wrong because I could tell something was. She was already angry with me before supper. It began while my sister and brother-in-law were visiting here for about an hour. She told me tonight that she didn't like me "bringing these people in here and sitting and talking to them." She said she didn't know what we were saying, and that bothered her. Also she said she didn't like me "bringing all these kids in here" and all the noise I make. We usually watch TV only for about an hour before bedtime. I know that she sometimes thinks the people on TV are real, and though she usually enjoys what we watch, there are times when the "kids" and "people" bother her.

We didn't stay in bed long tonight. I think I got between thirty minutes and an hour of sleep. We were up by 8:30 p.m. My mother sat in her chair and stared at me, not falling asleep till around 10:30 p.m. I hear her breathing and mumbling in her sleep as she often does—probably having a dream. I hope it's a good one.

Monday, February 6, 1995

I was pleasantly surprised on Saturday night. We went back to bed at midnight to sleep until daylight. Again, this morning, another nice surprise. I thought my mother was getting up to stay up at 6:30 a.m., when she went to use the bathroom in the other side of the house, but she went back to bed to stay till 7:30 a.m. It was so nice to stay in bed that late.

When she did get up, my mother complained of pain—a headache, neck ache, and as I suspected, indigestion. I gave her something for the headache first. She didn't want to come to the table for breakfast but said she might eat a few bites if I would bring it to her. She ate only a little, and still complained of hurting, so I gave her something for indigestion.

She was still in her gown when the Home Health aide came to give her a bath. By 9:30 a.m. she seemed to be feeling well again, and we've had a nice day. I've read two magazine stories to her, and she seemed to enjoy them. Now at 2:00 p.m., she has fallen asleep again, resting peacefully in her chair.

Wednesday, February 15, 1995

We've had such good days and nights for over a week now that I haven't felt the need to write in this journal. Everything has gone so well that I really thought I was making wonderful progress at learning how to take care of my mother and get along with her. Then bang—reality again…

Less than two hours ago my mother held hands with me as we watched TV. She gave me the biggest hug before I helped her into bed. It was a little later than usual for her to go to bed, so I thought surely she would sleep well most of the night. She has surprised me now at 9:30 p.m., nearly knocking me out of the way as she headed straight for her chair, refusing to let me help her into her robe, saying she "wished they had got anybody but some of Mama's people" to stay with her. I think tonight I am a distant relative on her mother's side of the family. Her reason for getting up: "That old bed was killing me!" At least it isn't very cold tonight. We are having a severe thunderstorm—that could be the problem.

We had such good times the past few days. My mother has really seemed to enjoy it when I've read to her from **Reader's Digest** (Pleasantville, NY), from **Guideposts** (Carmel, NY), even some from a book about Laura Ingalls Wilder. Yesterday I gave her some Valentine's Day presents—a little bag of candy, a sweatshirt I'd painted for her, and a card. She seemed so proud of them, showing them off to my sister when she came.

My mother was so worried about me just before bedtime. I wasn't feeling well—indigestion—and I had told my mother to help her understand it's something everyone has sometimes so maybe she wouldn't think she was dying whenever it happened to her. She told me she didn't know what she would do if something happened to me. And now she wishes I had never come.

She is sleeping in her chair now. The memory loss is a blessing as well as a curse. When she awakes, she probably won't remember her anger towards me. I hope not, anyway.

Saturday, February 18, 1995

We were up the rest of the night Wednesday night, and we've been up most of this night, too, but my mother has been calm, though she didn't want to put her robe on, and it's a bit too chilly tonight to go without one. At 3:00 a.m. she decided to go back to bed, but she got up again about a half-hour later. She's been friendly with me, and we even had a snack of soda crackers together. Once later when she awoke from sleeping in her chair, she said something like "I couldn't sleep much when I went back to bed with her." Then after a bathroom visit, she started to go to the kitchen and then stopped, saying "I guess she's not got breakfast ready yet." It's a bit early, but I guess it's time for me to start breakfast.

Friday, February 24, 1995

My mother's appointment with her neurologist was yesterday. I learned about some things I should be doing with my mother, though I'm not so sure some of them will work well. The doctor encouraged me to try to get her to be more active, to stay awake more, to exercise. She also said I should try to get her to sit up straight, and that, I really doubt I can do, as my mother's poor posture in her chair is a habit she has developed over many years. I have also learned that in all my cutting down on fat and lowering my mother's cholesterol, I've lowered her protein intake too much—this we learned from the blood tests that Home Health has been doing. I've got to do better—got to get it all right.

Saturday, February 25, 1995

We were up much of the night last night and again tonight—very early—starting at 8:00 p.m. My mother is so confused tonight. She keeps talking, telling me that I need to get a job. I think tonight she thinks I'm someone who has moved in with her, taking advantage of her for room and board, living off her. She has also just accused me of staying up all hours of the night and bothering her.

When morning comes, I will have my day off for shopping and attending my monthly Alzheimer's support group meeting. I wish I could get a little sleep, but at least I will have a day away. My sister will be here with my mother. It's strange that my mother never complains to my sister about me. She always complained about her sitters who had been hired to stay with her. But when I'm gone, my sister says that my mother just worries, afraid that I've gone away and won't come back. She has also worried, though, that I have taken her money with me.

CHAPTER 6

▼

SEEING THINGS

What's Wrong?

What's wrong? I ask my mother
a dozen times a day,
when I see that worried look,
and I fear what she will say.
It's usually just a dream
that seems to her so real,
she thinks something's got to be done.
things are just not right, she feels.
I tell her again it's just a dream;
There's no need to worry; all is well.
After a dozen times of hearing that
her frown begins to fade.
Relaxed, she falls asleep again,
back into her dream-filled day.
And I wait and hope
her dreams will be pleasant this time,
or they will be forgotten,
erased from her mind.

Thursday, March 2, 1995

I'm so scared, I'm literally shaking now. It seems I have only a few days to recover from one bad time, and then we have another.

Saturday turned out all right after all. Sometime between 3:00 a.m. and 4:00 a.m., my mother decided to go back to bed, so I got about three hours of sleep, and everything was fine on my day off. Well, everything except that at the Alzheimer's support group meeting everyone was telling me that I have to have help, that I couldn't go on without sleep, that I had to get my sister to spend the night sometimes so I could sleep, or that we had to hire someone else. None of those are solutions. My sister had over a year and a half of sleepless nights already before I came home, and she has a job and a family. Not having to hire someone is why I came home, and because my mother was always complaining about those who were hired to take care of her, and because only one of them was ever able to handle taking care of her for more than a few weeks or months.

Anyway, after a good morning when she complimented my breakfast, after a nap, my mother awoke all upset, scared, and confused. When I tried to calm her, she told me that I wasn't supposed to be here, that she didn't want me touching anything in the kitchen, or putting any clothes in the dryer, or putting my mail in the mail box. She was so afraid I would disturb "the other girl's things". Trying to talk to her about it, trying to reassure her that everything was all right, only made her more agitated. All I could do was leave her alone for a while.

Friday, March 4, 1995

It's 2:30 a.m. My mother just got up to sit in her chair, probably for the rest of the night, since wanting to ever since 9:00 p.m. Since then I've kept her in bed by telling her it was either before or just after midnight. Even at her 9:00 p.m. try, though, she was angry, and as she got back into bed she said that she was going to talk to someone about getting rid of me. Her words were mumbled and garbled, but I think I heard her say she was going to talk to her mother.

Monday, March 6, 1995

Sometimes I think I'm doing better with my mother, when I look back over the first six months of my journal. We had some terrible times in the first few months. In some ways, things are much easier now compared to then. She does eat most of the time, she's not as incontinent now as she was then, and when she gets up at night, she doesn't usually wander all through the house looking for "the baby", or "U.S." (my father), or "home". She does get up more in the middle of the night now (the frequency is increasing every month), but when she does, she usually just goes to sit in her chair. She gets confused, more often I think, upon getting up whether in the mornings or at night, and even throughout the day. It's mostly just verbal now, not physical. She hasn't raised her hand to hit me in a long time. But there is a lot of anger in her words. This morning she told me that she thinks I'm so awful and that I had "run off all the other girls that were here."

She had been talking about "the chickens" this morning when she got up, and when I told her everything was alright, she didn't have to worry about any chickens, she said "I don't know what to do, and you don't either!" I tried to help her get her robe on, but she wouldn't let me, and when I put her wrap over her legs after she sat in her chair, she told me, very angrily, "Leave me alone!" After I got breakfast ready and came for her, she mumbled something about needing to take something "to the train." I told her everything was ok and she had probably just had a dream. Again, I made the mistake of saying something like that; and this was when she told me how awful I was.

It's a dark cloudy day, and that doesn't help. Three more days of rain are forecast before we're to have a day that is only partly cloudy. Spring is arriving outside, though. I hope, if we can ever get outside again, the flowers I'm planting will cheer my mother.

Wednesday, March 8, 1995

What is it about my being here that makes my mother get up in the middle of the night and sit up all night the way she does? She didn't do it this way when my sister stayed with her at night. Is this another stage of the disease, or is this happening because I'm allowing it, or am I doing something that is causing it to happen?

My mother stayed in bed only three hours tonight, and telling her we needed to stay there longer so we'd both feel better the next day did no good. She informed me that she was leaving here as soon as her Mama came to get her because she didn't like this place.

We had a strange night last night, too. My mother was incontinent for the first time in several months. It was really my fault—I didn't wake up soon enough, and she was sitting on the side of her bed when it happened.

Again, later in the night she got up and I didn't hear her. She was all the way in the other side of the house, sitting in her chair in the dark, and I don't know how long she had been there. This doesn't happen often—usually I'm awake as soon as I hear her move, but sometimes when I'm really tired it happens, and I feel so bad when it does, because who knows what could happen to her wandering around alone in the house.

Thursday, March 9, 1995

We got lucky last night, and my mother stayed up only an hour longer and then we went back to bed. She did get up again an hour later to go to the bathroom in the other side of the house, and she said she was looking for someone, so I was afraid we would be staying up again, but we didn't.

This morning my mother got up at 5:00 a.m, didn't want her robe on or a wrap over her legs, didn't want me to fix her any breakfast, and she said her parents were coming to get her for a day in town. By the time I got breakfast about ready, she wanted to go back to bed. She ate just a little cream of wheat first and then went back to bed and slept about thirty to forty-five minutes. When she got up again, she allowed me to help her get dressed, but she was behaving strangely. After a nap in her chair, she seemed to be in pain, so I gave her something for her headache. Then she grabbed her chest and throat, so I thought it was indigestion and gave her something for that. A little later she started shaking as if she might be having a seizure, and she didn't seem to be able to talk. I called the Home Health nurse. A few minutes later, my mother got up and started walking around and seemed ok except for still acting kind of strange, so I called to Home Health to tell them I thought she was ok, but the nurse was already on the way.

By the time the nurse arrived, the shaking had started again, though not as much as earlier, and that plus a slightly elevated blood pressure made the nurse insist that we shouldn't take any chances, so we called 911, got my sister off work, and had the ambulance take my mother to the emergency room.

We were there several hours with a heart monitor hooked up, chest x-rays taken, blood tests, and everything came out fine—nothing at all wrong, according to the tests. The doctor gave us a prescription for something for gastritis. And I've probably caused the gastritis by giving my mother foods high in protein because the previous blood tests had showed her protein being low. No matter how hard I try to do the right things, sometimes it seems like I just can't do anything right in taking care of my mother.

Tuesday, March 14, 1995

We've been doing so well lately—almost a full week now of sleeping all night, and even till past daylight. I was hoping maybe this meant that the getting up all during the night was over. But we're had another one last night. At 11:30 p.m. my mother said, "I just couldn't stay there any longer". Before that every time I'd got up with her for a bathroom visit she had been so sweet and told me, "You don't have to get up with me. Just stay in bed."

We had a such a nice afternoon yesterday. She wanted to sit outside and watch me work in the flowers. I got the bench for the garden ready for her over the weekend with some help from my brother-in-law, and she loves it. We sat out there for a while, and she watched me plant flowers around the tree by the bench. It was a wonderful afternoon.

I had hoped things were really getting better—that maybe the Zantac® the doctor prescribed, the Mylanta® he said to give her, and a change in her diet would help the stomach problems so well that she would begin sleeping all night. But it's not just a stomach problem that's making her confused, though that may worsen it—my mother has Alzheimer's, and that's not going to get any better.

At supper my mother got that worried look on her face and started asking strange questions: "I didn't marry him?" and then "Who did I marry?" She was so relieved and happy for a while to learn who she had married, that she had not married the other one who she almost married, the one who drank a lot.

The other day she got so worried in the afternoon and when I noticed and asked why, I found it was because my brother was here, getting his tractor that was stored in an old chicken house. My mother heard the noise and asked what was happening. When I told her, she said he was going to get in trouble, that he was stealing, taking what belonged to "that man". I tried to explain to her that it was William's own tractor and that he was just storing it in the old chicken house, but I don't think I eased her worry any. Only forgetting what she was worrying about would do that.

I think she is hallucinating more. She sees people in the TV set even when it's not turned on (a reflection of herself, perhaps), she sees birds at the feeders when they aren't there, sometimes she even sees the bird feeders as people. Tree stumps in the pasture are cows or pigs, and tall grass or short trees at a distance become people. Inside, a pillow or a shadow can become a person. The arm of her chair, her leg wrap, or the covers on her bed can become a baby. Anyone who comes in can become either a dear old school friend or a hated enemy.

There are times, too, when she seems to have lost her ability to talk at all—when she just grunts and seems to be trying to talk but can't. It scares me every time, because I think it may be a larger stroke or a permanent loss of function. It happened last Thursday before we took her to the emergency room. And it happened again today for a little while.

Thursday March 16, 1995

It's 1:00 a.m., and we've been up for a few minutes now. My mother has wanted to get up since midnight, but I told her I needed to warm up this side of the house, that I was afraid the change in temperature would make her sick. This time I think she understood because she went back to bed for a while.

Yesterday was a strange day—hallucinations most of the day. In the afternoon I was out of the house for a few minutes, and I heard a noise. I rushed back in and saw she had turned over her water glass, spilling the water, and was about to pour some milk in my glass of diet cola. She said she was "getting milk for that kid that came crying" to her. I got another glass and poured a little milk, because I knew that telling her there was no kid there would not go over well. She took the glass of milk and went looking all over the house for "the kid", and not finding one, she put the glass of milk in the refrigerator.

It was much the same earlier yesterday and all afternoon—she saw people everywhere, said she didn't like this house, that she wanted to find her a house by herself, that she needed a real farm, said she was going to go with the next man who came along, marry him, to get away from here. If it weren't all so sad and so hard to deal with at the moment, there's so much humor in things she says at times—if I could just feel relaxed, maybe I could enjoy the humor.

I finally retreated to the kitchen, telling her I was going to finish cooking dinner. By the time dinner was over, she was ok, for a little while. We're still up at 4:30 a.m. Soon it will be time to fix breakfast. My mother seemed to have indigestion around 3:00 a.m., and I gave her some Mylanta®. I'm glad we've found out that and the Zantac® seem to work—at least, I hope they are working.

Saturday, March 18, 1995

We've been up since 2:00 a.m. with my mother insisting that breakfast had to be fixed for "them" right away. This time I couldn't get her to go back to bed until I could turn on the heaters and warm the house up. (If only I can, sometimes I can succeed in tricking her—If I can just get her to go back to bed, she will fall asleep and forget whatever it was she thought she was getting up to do.)

I didn't start breakfast then because my contact lenses were out and in cleaning solution. I tried to explain that and got her settled in her chair. I nervously tried to get my contacts in quickly, dropping one and almost losing it on the floor twice. When I got them back in and was ready to fix breakfast as she wanted me to do, my mother was asleep in her chair.

My sister told me that once while my dad was alive, my mother got up and cooked breakfast, had it ready at 3:00 a.m. and tried to get my dad up to eat it at that time. When he asked why she did it, she said, "I didn't even look at the clock and just thought it was time to get up." My dad died ten years ago, and this was long before then. My sister and I think our mother had Alzheimer's then, or perhaps it began even further back than that. We can think of things she did—early symptoms even as far back as twenty years ago.

Last night when she went to bed, my mother was saying she thought she was going to die. She said she wasn't hurting anywhere, no indigestion, no headaches, but she just felt like she wasn't going to live much longer. Though she was about to go to sleep when I got her dressed for bed, she lay awake for an hour, whispering prayers apparently.

Then at 9:00 p.m., she started getting up about every half-hour to use the bathroom. Each time she was confused about something she had dreamed—thinking it was real. Someone had accused her of something she didn't do, one of her kids had got married and that would be one less to cook for. I can't remember the other things, but she kept saying "they said" and things she had apparently dreamed about. It seemed she didn't hear or understand anything I said to her, and when she climbed back into bed she was saying "But they said…" How I wish I could turn off her ability to have dreams—I wish there was some drug that would prevent them. She dreams someone is in the bedroom with us, and she believes it so strongly, it's like when she wakes up she still sees him or her there.

Alzheimer's is a strange and amazing disease. Some people actually thought I would be bored coming back to the country to take care of my mother with no cable TV and no computer with Internet access. I would like to have the computer for finding information and support as a caregiver, but it's definitely not boring around here!

Sunday, March 19, 1995

My mother was up before midnight again last night. I tried to encourage her to stay in bed a little longer; told her we both needed some sleep. She told me she was "getting sick of hearing about sleep" and that she "didn't know how anyone could sleep when one of the kids is out there..." The rest of it was mumbled and I couldn't understand what she was saying—something from one of her dreams, something she thought was happening to one of her kids, apparently. No amount of telling her "It was just a dream" would do any good at all.

Sometimes it seems the bad nights come after we have some very good days. Yesterday was so nice, the weather was so warm, and we took a couple of long walks, sat on the porch for a while, sat on the bench in the garden for a while. It seems that all of that should make the night better, but it didn't.

We did get some sleep yesterday morning, though. After sitting up from 1:00 a.m. until 4:30 a.m., my mother decided to go back to bed. We slept until 7:30 a.m.—and that was so wonderful!

Wednesday, March 22, 1995

Monday was the first day of Spring, but my mother didn't want to go outside all day. She slept a lot during the day. Today she was wide-awake all morning, walking through the house, and we took several walks outside. She said she felt so good. She ran out of energy in the afternoon and took a short nap, but she didn't sleep as much as some days. We're still getting up at night, whether she is more active in the daytime or not, it doesn't seem to matter. Tonight we are already up at 10:30 p.m.

Friday, March 24, 1995

Last night we were watching an episode of "Little House on the Prairie" (NBC, 1975-1982) on a video, and my mother suddenly got that worried look. I stopped the tape and asked her what was wrong. She said she hadn't done right by "Sue" (My middle name and what she always called me), that she didn't know where "Sue" was, and that she was worried about her. I tried to explain to her that I am Sue, that she hadn't done anything to me and that I wasn't missing, that I'd been right here with her for six months. She wouldn't accept it, didn't understand me, whatever—she just kept repeating what she had said, worrying about "Sue".

This is the hardest thing about Alzheimer's—the most maddening thing. Whenever she remembers she has a daughter by my name, she thinks she's somewhere else, and she worries about her—not understanding or not accepting that I've been right here with her all along.

Wednesday, March 29, 1995

We had a pleasant surprise Sunday night. My mother was up at 9:00 p.m., and I was sure it would be another all-nighter, but she went back to bed half an hour later.

Another very nice surprise Monday night—she slept all night until 5:30 a.m. That was wonderful!

But this morning we were up at 3:00 a.m. Not only was she up then, but she was tugging at the covers on her bed, pulling them all off onto the floor, before I could get myself awake.

I must be getting Alzheimer's too—already. I fixed breakfast at 3:00 a.m. myself! I had set one of the clocks wrong and thought it was 4:00 a.m. I thought we had actually stayed in bed till it was about time to get up (or as late as I could usually expect my mother to sleep).

Thursday, March 30, 1995

We may have just had our biggest catastrophic reaction ever. I had just got back into bed half an hour ago and was sound asleep (it's only 8:30 p.m.). When my mother got up, I tried a little harder than usual to get her to go back to bed since it was so early and we hadn't been there long. She got angry with me and refused her robe when I tried to help her put it on. When I tried a second time (my mistake) she sure woke me up fast—by some hard slaps in the face!

Yes, she can hit. She is strong, and she can hurt! She called me "Hateful thing!" I think it had something to do with the "babies" she was dreaming about or seeing in her hallucination. According to her, I was supposed to be taking care of them, and I wasn't fulfilling my duties. Apparently she woke up, found me sleeping, and was already angry because I wasn't doing my job.

She's already asleep in her chair now, and I'm watching from the next room. I was afraid she would come looking for me after I left her in her chair, but she didn't. When she wakes up, hopefully she will have forgotten. I'm always so afraid she will remember incidents, or remember them incorrectly. The way things get all backwards in her mind sometimes, she may have thought I hit her instead of her hitting me.

Friday, March 31, 1995

Everything turned out fine last night. My mother had forgotten by midnight, and she was as sweet as could be. She got out of her chair, and though I couldn't understand what she was saying, she seemed very pleasant toward me. Somehow while talking we made it back to the bedroom and she went back to bed.

She tried to get up around 3:00 a.m., but I told her as gently as I could "I won't argue with you about it anymore, no matter what time it is. But I do need to make sure it's warm first so you won't catch cold." So she got back in bed so I could go turn the heaters on, and she slept until 4:30 a.m.

My mother was silent during breakfast, silent while I was helping her change her clothes, and she was soon in silent sleep in her chair where she still is. I sometimes wonder if she can remember anything at all about the night before. I doubt she can remember much, because she can't remember from one minute till the next. If she can remember anything, it's probably bits and pieces and perhaps a feeling that something happened, that something's not quite right. But then again, perhaps that's the way someone with Alzheimer's feels all the time.

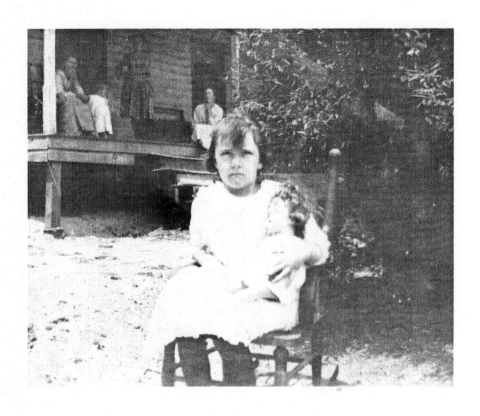

My mother as a little girl holding a doll, about 1924

My parents, Ulysses S. Parris and Jessie Lee Dempsey Parris

They were married in December 1934.

She was eighteen and he was thirty-four.

They were still a handsome couple in 1959 when I was five years old…

and in 1976 when I was in my third year of college.

Proud grandmother with her first grandchild, my niece, Bethany Dawn Allen.
Dawn is my sister Myrtle's oldest child, and this photo was made about 1968.

CHAPTER 7

▼

BIRTHDAY BLUES

Mama's Baby

You cared for me, perhaps
too much—I was a bit spoiled.
I'm sure you must have
cried when I got married.
And when I got divorced,
you had a stroke.
You pleaded with me
to come home, so I did.
Mama's baby came home,
but you don't know me.
I'm too late—
Alzheimer's came first.

Saturday, April 1, 1995

No April-fooling—it's been some bad morning!

My mother got over her confused morning yesterday and seemed okay until just before lunch when she started asking how she got here, why was she brought here, telling me that she didn't need to be here, she wasn't sick, why didn't her family come? It took taking her outside and walking around the house to convince her that she hadn't left home (or to distract her so that she would forget her concern).

The same thing had happened just a day or two ago, and I had to get my sister to come and talk to her, because she was getting angry with me for "bringing" her "here".

Last night was ok till 2:00 a.m., and then she was babbling, not saying anything I could understand at all. I got her robe on her and she sat in her chair for a few minutes, then she went back to bed to stay just till 3:00 a.m. She was cheerful then and even thanked me for helping her when I put her robe on her and got her seated in her chair again.

When she woke up, she was so confused that she got mixed up about which to use to wash her hands—the sink or the commode. Luckily, I caught her just in time, and helped her (and I will never let her wash her hands unsupervised again—she often can't figure out how to turn the water on anyway), but I think my panic at what she was about to do confused her further.

At breakfast, she took only a bite and then said that she wasn't eating anything, that it was poison, that she "had seen it", that "it was going to kill everybody, kill all the children", that she wasn't "going to eat anything else in this house."

I got her to drink her orange juice and coffee and (to my surprise) to take her medicine. But when I was trying to explain (will I ever completely quit trying to explain?) that there was nothing wrong with the food, that I bought it and fixed it myself, she got so angry that she began pushing and hitting.

There was also the first bowel incontinence today. Actually it was a matter of going to the bathroom by herself when I wasn't watching and not realizing she needed to pull down her pants. She was pulling them up from the legs. I have tried to watch her carefully and go to help her in the bathroom every time, but she can move so fast and silently, even when I think I'm watching her close enough.

I have decided that this is it. I'm not going to be able to do this anymore. My sister keeps asking, keeps saying she's ready anytime I am, so I'm going to let her get my mother on a nursing home waiting list.

Sunday, April 2, 1995

I told my sister we'd had some problems, but I didn't mention the nursing home, and I only told her about the incontinence, which I said I could handle by just watching my mother more closely and asking her more often about going to the bathroom. I didn't tell her about the hitting—just told her Mother had been angry—but she knows, because it happened to her—much more than it has to me so far.

We had a good night last night, except for something that happened around 8:30 p.m. that left me sleepless and tossing in my bed for a while. Just about an hour after going to bed, my mother got up and started leaving the room. I tried to get her to stay, because it was still so early. Then giving in, I got her robe and tried to put it on her, but she pushed me away. She said she was just going to fix some dinner, and then she was going back to bed.

She went to the stove and found two muffins I'd made yesterday and started trying to get them out of the zip-lock bag. I tried to help her, and she pushed me away again and raised her hand to hit me. I realized she didn't have her dentures in and that she couldn't eat the muffin without them, so tried to get her to put them in—and again, more pushing and threatened slaps. She said she had her teeth in already, and she took the muffin to the living room, breaking it in little pieces and eating it without her dentures, saying all the time that she was going to eat this dinner if it was the last thing she did. After she finished eating it, I tried to give her a glass of water, but she refused. Having crumbs all over her nightgown, she tried to take the gown off. I said "Mama, honey, don't take your gown off", and then there was more pushing and a hand raised as if to slap me. I followed her back into the bedroom and tried to get her covered up after she got in the bed, but she wouldn't let me. Every time I tried to pull the covers up over her, she slapped at me and told me to get away and leave her alone. She said she was going to talk to "that man" about getting rid of me.

I gave up on getting covers over her and just turned on the heat until about an hour later when I knew she was asleep. Then I pulled a blanket up over her. I lay there awake for at least two hours, maybe more, fearing that she would awake and we would have more to go through before the night was over. Finally I fell asleep, and then she awoke, but she was nice and cooperative. She used the bathroom and went right back to bed, as sweet as could be.

And wonder of wonders, she slept until 6:00 a.m. this morning. Well, actually only till 5:00 a.m., if it weren't for today being the first day of daylight savings time. I guess it's good she can no longer tell time, or she might have insisted we get up an hour early.

When she did awake again, my mother was talking about fixing dinner. I told her I would get breakfast fixed right away. When I had it ready, she refused to go to wash her hands and come to the table.

She said it was "too early", and mumbled something like she didn't "want to go". I left her alone, got myself dressed, and brought breakfast to her on a tray. She ate, and she said her reason for not doing so before was, that she was "just waiting to see what ya'll were going to do."

Something strange happened last night at supper, too. As I was washing the dishes, she told me her mother was really old and sick and she was afraid she was going to have to quit school and take care of her. She asked me how much longer I had in school. Then she asked "Am I not in school?", and when I said "No.", she just said "Oh."

Everything was fine as we went to watch "Little House on the Prairie" (NBC, 1975-1982) which is usually safe. (The previous night had Jesse and Frank James in it, and that wasn't a good one to watch.) She laughed at Mrs. Olsen throughout the show, and she was in a good mood at bedtime.

Monday, April 3, 1995

It's 2:00 a.m., and we just got up. It's chilly in the house, but I couldn't get my mother to stay in bed just a little while longer so I could turn the heaters on. At least she did let me put her robe on her and her wrap over her legs. I've learned the less I protest her getting up, the less angry she gets. So if she says no once to my request that she go back to bed, then that's fine—it's time for us to get up.

Getting her to Sunday dinner yesterday went well. She woke up confused, but she seemed to understand when we talked about it as I served her a snack. Then I said we would take a walk in a few minutes. We did, and I guided the walk up towards my sister's house, showing my mother the flowers all the way there. She didn't protest at all when we arrived at the door, and then I told her we had been invited there for Sunday dinner.

She's confused about something now. She was mumbling just now about "that man." But I've found again and again that it's pointless to try to explain anything to her. I've got her settled in her chair and I've moved to the next room where I can watch her.

At the last Alzheimer's support group meeting I borrowed a video that is helping me understand more of what is happening. As the Alzheimer's affects more of the brain, the hallucinations will increase—not only visual hallucinations, but auditory as well. In the past few days that has been happening a lot. My mother asks something about what she thinks has been said even when nothing has been said at all.

My sister and I had a talk yesterday and I told her everything. Even before I did, she was encouraging me to just say the word and we would have our mother put in the nursing home. I told her how important it is to me to keep on taking care of my mother through the summer, how my minimum goal is a year, how I've got to try it for at least four and a half more months, that the closer I get to that year with my mother, the better I will feel, the more I will feel that my time here wasn't worthless, a waste, and I a failure.

Now at 3:30 a.m., my mother has just gone back to bed after being up and wandering around the house for half an hour. She was feeling the wrap she had taken from her legs, and then feeling the arm of her chair and saying there was a dead man there. She was in such a panic about it, pacing through the house, saying something had to be done. Finally she wore herself out, and I led her back to the bedroom. As she crawled into bed, I told her I was going to turn the light out, and she said "You'd better do something about that poor old dead man, too." I assured her that I would.

I went back to bed but couldn't go back to sleep. She got up at 5:00 a.m. As I was fixing breakfast, she started looking confused. She ate most of her breakfast, but she didn't say a word. At times it was like she was trying to say something but couldn't. After breakfast, she took me back to the bedroom to show me. She thought someone was in her bed. I turned on the light and moved the covers to show her there was no one there. She went to sit in her chair, but she began acting like she couldn't get her breath and shaking like she did the day the nurse insisted she be taken to the emergency room.

I assumed that she had indigestion, but I wasn't sure what to do since antacids weren't supposed to be taken within an hour before or after Zantac®, which she'd taken just before breakfast. I called my sister, and she said to give her a glass of water first. Halfway through the water, my mother got up to go to the bathroom, and she felt better after that. I think that she just needed to have a bowel movement and didn't realize what was wrong.

Since then she's been so different every time she awakens from her naps. The first time she was feeling great and in a really good mood. The last time she woke up she said that she was hurting, but she said she had already taken some medicine and that it didn't work, and she went on to say that nothing did.

Tuesday, April 4, 1995

Last night was great except for one terrifying incident a couple of hours after my mother went to bed. She got up, asking where Sue was. I told her

I was Sue, and she just went on asking and saying she was so worried. Every time I would tell her I was Sue, she would get madder and madder, even using a bad word twice. I had never ever heard my mother say such a thing before till a couple of months ago, and then I still wasn't quite sure I had heard it.

I saw I wasn't going to get her calmed down, so I called my sister, and she and her husband came and talked to her for about an hour or so till they got her calmed down and back in bed.

She didn't wake up again to go to the bathroom until 4:00 a.m., and I had to look at the clock a second time because I couldn't believe she had stayed in bed that long. She went back to bed then and slept for another hour. Breakfast went smoothly except that she kept on stirring her cream of wheat instead of eating it. I kept telling her it had been stirred enough and that she just needed to eat it. She would eat a few bites, and then she would be stirring it again and again. Finally she forgot about stirring it and finished off the bowl.

Saturday, April 8, 1995

We're up at 1:00 a.m., but that's better than 10:30 p.m., when my mother had tried to get up earlier, but I talked her out of it.

Her seventy-ninth birthday was Thursday. She wasn't too excited about the cake and presents at first, but she did try to blow out the candles. I asked her later if she'd had a good birthday. She said "yes", and for a minute I thought I saw just a glimmer of happiness and gratitude.

Wednesday, April 12, 1995

The last few nights have been great, and I have become spoiled. I keep hoping when we have a few good nights that maybe the sleepless nights are over for good. But no such luck. And as for luck, tonight is the night I took my contact lenses out, and I am blind as a bat but can't put them back in for several hours. We are up at 11:00 p.m.

Thursday, April 13, 1995

Now at 2:15 a.m., I can retreat to my nook in the next room now that I have my contacts back in. I had to sit in the same room with my mother until I got them back in, because I was afraid I wouldn't see her if she got up from her chair.

I am wide awake now, but nauseous after a glass of diet cola, a cup of tea, a cup of coffee, and a caffeine pill.

Friday, April 14, 1995

At 6:25 p.m. tonight my mother wanted to go to bed. At 6:30 p.m. she got angry with me for taking her to bed. She said she couldn't sleep on "that old hard bed" and that she wanted to sleep in her "other bed" (her chair).

I told her that if she would just sleep in bed for a couple of hours till I got that much sleep, then I would be ok and we could get up. She got really angry then, said that she was going to talk to "that man", going to talk to Myrtle (my sister), going to find someone good to stay with her.

I said ok, I would leave if that was what she wanted, we would take care of it tomorrow, would tell Myrtle then.

She told me I should sleep in the daytime. I told her that I had to cook then, clean the house, wash her clothes. She told me that, I didn't do anything, that I cooked hardly anything, and so on.

She got into bed, but she kept tossing and turning and raising up to look at me. So I said ok, she could get up if she would let me help her put on her robe, and we got up for another night.

Saturday, April 15, 1995

I made several mistakes last night before I got my mother back into bed around 9:30 p.m. Around 7:30 p.m. she went back to the bedroom and sat on the side of the bed but didn't get into bed. I sat down to talk to her, and she was apologetic but said she couldn't believe she had really said those things to me. She kept on saying that so much, and I tried to tell her why. We've never made any attempt to keep the truth from her—that she has Alzheimer's.

To get her mind off it, I thought maybe we could watch another video. It held her attention. It made both of us sleepy enough to go back to bed, but perhaps a movie that late added to her confusion. Mistake number two was giving her a second Thoridazine® just before she went back to bed.

Just before 2:00 a.m. she was incontinent. While I was clumsily making an attempt to change the sheets and watch after her too, she told me that she would go back to bed when I got it ready. When I finally got it ready, she wouldn't go back, nor would she put on her robe, nor her wrap over her legs. The house was chilly, so I turned the heat up high for a little while.

Mistake number three: The well pump was running and there was no water after my putting the sheets on to wash. I had been told that the pump could burn up if it kept running like that, when there was no water coming through. I had forgotten where the switch was down in the cellar for turning the pump off. So I called my sister in the middle of the night again.

She came, and my brother-in-law came with her and turned off the switch. She sat and talked to my mother for a few minutes only to hear "That woman thinks she owns this house!" My sister didn't have her usual success at getting her to go back to bed. I apologized and told my sister and her husband to go on home and back to bed. She was reluctant, but I told her this was something I would just have to wait out.

Just before my sister had arrived, my mother had said "You can take your baby and leave!" I don't know what caused that one. An earlier movie last night (not the latter one), had got her a little upset because of some loud noise—and it was one of her favorite movies—a Shirley Temple. Perhaps she had remembered something from that, and it caused all the confusion? I keep thinking that we may have to completely stop watching movies. She seems to enjoy them so much at times, but I never know when any part of a movie may get her confused and upset.

Sunday, April 16, 1995

My mother got up again last right after going to bed. She went back to bed at 9:30 p.m., but she got up again at 10:00 p.m. and wandered around the house. She was convinced there was someone else in the house, some child I was not taking care of, I think, and it took turning on all the lights and walking through the house several times to convince her otherwise. Then she sat in her chair and fell asleep.

At about 3:30 a.m. this morning I was so sleepy I just couldn't stay awake any longer. I lay down on the couch in the next room, in a position from which I could still see her but she couldn't see me. I just lay there watching, but did doze off around 4:00 a.m. As soon as I fell asleep, she was up out of her chair, picking up her wrap, looking at it, turning it over and saying something about giving "this ice cream to the little boy". I tried to find out what she wanted, to play along with it this time. She said the ice cream needed to be put up, that it would melt out here, so I took her wrap to the kitchen, but that didn't satisfy her. Then she said the little boy needed his breakfast, so I thought maybe she was saying it was breakfast time. I told her I would start breakfast and set a place for the little boy so he could eat. Then she said he wouldn't eat it, that he wanted ice cream. So I got her some ice cream, thinking she was meaning herself, but when I brought it to her, she said she couldn't give the little boy ice cream because she was crazy.

I told her she wasn't, and that she just had a disease that made her not remember and that confused her. I left her then, and watched from the next room again. Then she got up to go to the bathroom. I went to help her, and while there she told me that she wished someone would kill her, that she wanted to die. I tried to comfort her, to tell her how much she's loved. She said that things were just not right and that she wanted to do what was right but she just didn't know what to do. I told her that what was right for now would be going back to bed, that she would feel so much better if she would just lie down in bed and get some rest for at least an hour till breakfast time.

She did, and we slept till 7:00 a.m. She didn't look like she felt much better then, though. She ate most of her breakfast but she was silent.

After breakfast, I got her to go to the bathroom, saying we needed to get her Easter Sunday bath. After she used the bathroom, I guess what I had said sunk in. She refused the bath and said she wasn't going anywhere today. So I helped her get dressed, and she sat in her chair and slept for several hours.

I didn't think we would be spending Easter Sunday at my sister's, but we did make it, thanks to lovely warm sunny weather that allowed me to "trick" my mother into going by inviting her on a walk to see the flowers. She doesn't realize where we are going, and by the time we get to my sister's house, it's usually ok, and she enjoys the day once she gets there.

Monday, April 17, 1995

We were up last night before midnight, with my mother wandering through the house. She was looking for someone, and I couldn't figure out whom. Then she said something about her mother. Then she began talking about some money that needed to be paid to someone. As she sat in her chair, she asked if I had any money, and I told her "Yes, a little, and you can have it if you need it". Then she scolded me—I couldn't figure out why at first, and then it sounded like she was scolding me for letting someone borrow money, which she went on to tell me was why I had money problems. Then she said, "They said you'll have to wait till morning." I had told her earlier, when she was wandering through the house and talking about money, that no one was here and that whatever needed to be done about money could wait till morning. So she waited, but by sitting in her chair.

If it weren't for times like yesterday afternoon, I don't know if I could make it. We were all sitting in lawn chairs out under the trees in the backyard at my sister's. My brother insisted we switch chairs when he saw I was about to fall asleep in an upright chair. Once in the lounge chair, I promptly fell asleep.

Wednesday, April 19, 1995

We are up tonight at 11:00 p.m. The past few nights I've been giving my mother a cup of chamomile tea at bedtime, and I really think it's helped, but we ran out and she didn't have it tonight. The nights she did have her cup of tea, she got up more often to use the bathroom, but she just went right back to bed every time. Maybe I've found something that will really help.

Sunday, April 23, 1995

I've been getting so spoiled lately that if we get up an hour or two early, I think it's terrible. We've had some really good nights, sleeping all night long and even past daylight the next morning.

When I had my Alzheimer's support group meeting and shopping day yesterday I visited a health food store and got some herbal blends, with chamomile and other herbs that are supposed to promote relaxation and sleep. It seemed to help us both last night, though we were up at 3:00 a.m. My mother got up then saying "that other girl" told her it was time to get up.

Tuesday, April 25, 1995

Everything has been fine the last couple of days and nights. Today didn't start out well at all. My mother slept until 6:00 a.m., but she got up confused and angry. She asked me if I had gone to her parents' house, and I told her no and that I'd been right here with her. I watched her as I was fixing breakfast and saw that her anger was growing. So I stopped and went to ask her what was wrong, thinking maybe things would be better if we talked about it.

She said she wanted it stopped, that this was her house and she wanted all this carrying on, this tearing up things, this fighting stopped. I tried to tell her that she'd just had a bad dream, and then I went back to preparing breakfast, fearing that she wouldn't eat a bite when I got it ready.

Surprisingly, I was successful at getting her to eat and to take her medicine but not at getting her to believe me. Her confusion just seemed to grow as we talked all during breakfast. She said someone was trying to take her money, that there was a man here in bed with the girl that stayed with her. When I told her I was the girl who stayed with her, she asked, "Was that your husband in bed with you?"

I'm told not to correct her, but how do I not try to straighten her out about something like that? I can't let her think there's someone else here when having someone else here would make her frightened and angry like this.

We got through breakfast and changing clothes, but she was still confused and irritated with me. She took a little nap and when she woke up I asked her if she needed to go to the bathroom, and she said no. I peeked a minute later and saw she was on the way there. I went along to help, and she informed me that we were too late, it had happened already. This was our second time of bowel incontinence.

Afterwards she told me that "they" had given her something that had caused this. Then she told me she wanted "that thing for my hair", and I gave her a comb. We had got her hair just a bit wet in the shower, and she was upset about that, I think. She combed and combed her hair all forward in her face. Then she fell asleep in her chair.

Wednesday, April 26, 1995

We were up at 3:00 a.m. again, but at least it wasn't midnight or earlier. My mother got up extremely upset and asking why she had been taken to this place and where is Myrtle Lee (my sister, who she thinks is her sister), and something about some man. I got her settled in her chair and saw talking to her wasn't working, so I left her there and went to watch her from my spot in the next room.

I got lucky. We were up for only thirty minutes. She called me back to her and this time wanted to know why I got her out of bed. So we went back to bed and slept till 6:00 a.m.!

This morning my mother said breakfast was cold, and everything tasted terrible this morning, but some days are like that, I've learned.

CHAPTER 8

▼

FINALLY SPRING

Paradise

With the sound of leaves crunching
under our feet,
we walked through the garden
and sat on the bench.
The birds that were singing
sounded so sweet,
and the soft touch of the wind
felt good on my cheek.
It wasn't quite Eden
but it was as close
to paradise on earth
as I could hope.
Yes, she had Alzheimer's,
and yes, life was hard.
But we were in heaven,
just walking in the yard.

Monday, May 1, 1995

We were up at 3:30 a.m., but it seems like this isn't happening as often now and not as early in the night as it used to. We are much closer to getting full nights of sleep now. Still, I'm so sleepy when we get up a few hours before daylight. This morning I thought I would try lying on the couch to watch my mother, thinking maybe I could still get another nap or two.

It didn't work out that way. As soon as I fell asleep, she was up wandering through the house, saying everything was wrong and this was not her house. When I showed her the bed she sleeps in and the chair where she sits most of the time, she said "We have to get them out of here and back in my house."

We went through two hours of that, with her walking through the house and saying everything was wrong. Finally she settled in her chair, and I fixed breakfast. She came to the table but was still complaining about things being wrong and something needing to be done about it. She hardly touched her breakfast and refused her medicine.

I called my sister, got her out of bed and probably made her late for work, but she talked my mother through eating a little more of her breakfast and taking her medicine. She became more cooperative but still not happy. After breakfast I helped her with going to the bathroom and changing her clothes, and she settled down in her chair for a nap.

She woke up fine, just as peaceful as could be.

Thursday, May 4, 1995

My mother refused to eat and take her medicine again this morning. She also refused to let me help her change her clothes. I didn't call my sister this time, thinking that maybe my mother would get over it in a few hours.

I was right. When she woke up she was cooperative. But it seemed a little more life was gone from her. Most every time she has a catastrophic reaction, it seems like she's gone a little further after it, into a more advanced stage of Alzheimer's.

She has slept most of the day. It is a cloudy day, and that may be why. At lunch she had trouble eating. It was as if she couldn't remember how to use her spoon and tried to pick everything up with her fingers. I took her lunch to her on a tray because we were having a thunderstorm and I thought she might be afraid to eat in the kitchen. She has been very confused and what she has said hasn't made any sense all day. Once when I helped her with going to the bathroom she kept saying she didn't have any money and that she couldn't give me any. I kept trying to tell her I didn't want any of her money, that I didn't need anything. I think she's having auditory hallucinations, not understanding what I say and hearing something different from what I say.

Friday, May 5, 1995

We're up now at just after midnight. My mother got up at 10:00 p.m., but somehow I got her to go back to bed. I had to help her get back in bed, though. It was as if she had forgotten how.

Somehow lately she seems to have forgotten how to do a lot of little things. She can't remember how to use a spoon, or take out her dentures, and she walks in tiny steps, grasping my hand as if she's afraid she will fall. I can't understand much she says. She's seems to have forgotten how to use the bathroom, and she's afraid to sit on the commode or her bedside potty.

Yesterday afternoon she was shaking and said she was cold, but it wasn't cold in the house. I wrapped her up anyway. She was asleep when my sister came for a visit. We talked outside for a while. When we came back in, my mother was shaking again. My sister thought she might need food because she hadn't eaten much that day. So my sister helped her eat, feeding her with a spoon since she couldn't seem to manage it. Then my mother threw up. She must have a virus.

It's 7:45 a.m. now. I got my mother back to bed this morning at 4:30 a.m., and she stayed there until 6:00 a.m. She got up confused and talking about something that needed to be done, but I couldn't figure out what. She said she couldn't move and that she was waiting for "that woman" to help. Finally I got her to let me help her to her chair. I tried to feed her breakfast, but she spit out her toast and ate only about three teaspoons of cream of wheat. She wouldn't drink the soft drink my sister brought for her yesterday, thinking it might settle her stomach.

She let me help her to the bathroom, and then when we got back, she took a few small sips of orange juice. She said something like, "That woman said for me not to take it, and I'm not going to take it." I haven't tried to get her to take any medicine this morning, and I was only trying to get her to eat something, but she won't.

Just now at 8:15 a.m., I got her to take a few more sips of orange juice. She seemed better and was even able to hold her glass with a little help, but she still wouldn't drink much. I had better call Home Health and warn them, because I don't think they will be able to get her to take a bath today.

It's 10:50 a.m. The Home Health nurse said she was coming. Before I talked to Home Health, my mother had said she needed to go to the bathroom but she said she couldn't get up. So I had told Home Health that she seemed to have lost the ability to walk. I got out the bedside potty and helped my mother onto it, but she didn't use it. Later, before the nurse got here, we made a trip to the bathroom. My mother walked all the way there with help, and she used the bathroom for the first time today. After that, I also got her to drink a glass of juice, just before the nurse arrived.

The nurse checked her over, and she was fine as always, except for a slight temperature, and of course, gas in her stomach. The nurse said she probably had a virus. Just as she was leaving, the Home Health aide came to give my mother a bath. By that time she seemed to be feeling much better and the bath went fine.

After her bath, I got my mother to drink a half can of Ensure®. I will try some cream of chicken soup at lunch, and if that doesn't work, I'll give her more Ensure®, and maybe some ice cream, too.

Now it's 1:00 p.m. The chicken soup didn't work. My mother ate about four bites and said she'd had enough. I got her to drink most of the remaining Ensure®. But when I tried to get her to take a pill she spit it out. Now she's sleeping again and mumbling in her restless sleep.

When the nurse was here today she seemed more worried about me than about my mother, and she asked me if I had accepted the fact that my mother will never be well again and that she will only get worse. Of course I've accepted that she won't be well again, but the part I don't want to accept is that she will get worse. I need just a little more time with her. I'm not ready to let her go yet.

Saturday, May 6, 1995

We are up now at a little after midnight again, but my mother is very calm, and she's already had a full night's sleep. She went to bed really early—at 6:00 p.m., so really she and I both have had enough sleep.

She seems back to normal now and over being so sick. Yesterday when my sister arrived at 3:30 p.m., we peeped in where my mother had been sitting sleeping, and she was getting out of her chair all by herself. She was smiling and more herself again—even headed toward the front porch and sat out there in the swing for over an hour talking to my sister. Then for supper she ate a whole bowl of chicken soup, with a spoon all by herself, having no trouble at all. When I gave her the daily coated aspirin she's required to take, she did have difficulty swallowing that.

It seemed trying to swallow the pill got her a little upset. The Shirley Temple movie couldn't capture her attention, and she seemed to be either in pain or just very tired, so I gave her a Thoridazine® and got her ready for bed.

If my mother had permanently lost her mobility as I was afraid she had yesterday, I told my sister I would have said yes, that it was time for her to go to the nursing home. She is heavy, and I can't lift her, and surely couldn't at times when she might have struggled and fought me. But she's ok again now, and I will continue to take care of her, a few months more, a year, for however long I can manage.

It's 8:00 a.m. now. At about 3:30 a.m. my mother got up from her chair so confused and talking about a dead man. I didn't think she could see me where I had laid down on the couch in the next room, but I wonder if she did and if that's what caused the confusion this time. After talking for a while, she went to sleep again until 4:30 a.m. I saw her moving and went to ask if she needed something. She mumbled something which I thought sounded like "Let's go back to bed", so I took her to the bedroom, but once we were there, I discovered that wasn't what she meant. She went back to her chair and sat down, and I told her that when daylight came maybe the confusion would be gone and I would fix breakfast and every-thing would be fine then. She said, "Fix breakfast." I asked "now?", and she said "yes", so I did, though she fell asleep again while I was fixing it.

When she woke up she seemed fine. She ate half her breakfast and took a pill (Sinemet® for her Parkinson's symptoms). After breakfast, I got her dressed and she sat down in her chair. I asked her if everything was ok, because she looked a little worried about something. She said it would be when she got in the car. During the night she had said something about going "to the house" and I had told her I would take her wherever she wanted to go when daylight came. This time she obviously remembered that, and she wanted me to carry out the promise I made in the night. So from 7:00 a.m. to 7:30 a.m. this morning, I took her on a ride through town and back on the Interstate. When we got back, I told her she was home, and she seemed satisfied.

Sunday, May 7, 1995

Here we are again, right on schedule, and up just after midnight. This isn't the beginning for tonight, either. My mother sat on the side of her bed for two hours. She didn't want to go back to bed or to go to her chair—just sat there on her bed. The first hour it was without a robe, and I kept trying to get her to let me put it on her so she wouldn't get sick.

Finally she reached for it and let me help her put it on. She was talking about her daughter that had "got herself pregnant" (no such daughter has ever existed). Then my mother talked about "the man" she was married to, the "other U.S." she called him, and not the one who had died. She said he had gone to get some papers and she was waiting up till he got back.

I can't sit up awake this time. I know I will risk her being more confused if I fall asleep on the couch, but I just can't stay awake any longer, and I'm going to have to lie down on the couch.

Monday, May 8, 1995

My mother had a good day yesterday at my sister's while I was here cleaning house, gardening, and going grocery shopping—doing things that often upset my mother if I do them while she's here. She doesn't like for me to clean house while she's here, and it sometimes seems to upset her when I go shopping. It seems that sometimes she thinks I'm running up bills for her. She's better at my sister's when I'm not there, too. When I am there, often she keeps asking about going home, even when we've just got there.

Yesterday morning my mother had let me help her get back into bed at 3:30 a.m. Then she was up at 5:00 a.m., on the other side of my bed, shaking me to wake me up. I was so exhausted that this was one of the rare times when I didn't hear her get up.

She was so confused all morning, and she kept asking me so many questions that I could hardly get breakfast ready. She asked each of them all again as soon as I had answered them. It seemed that she'd forgotten or just got more mixed up every time I gave her an answer.

I called my sister at 8:00 a.m. and asked if I could bring my mother up early for Sunday dinner. My mother wanted to talk to her and see if she could answer her questions about the family, the past, and this house, for as my sister told me later, she though I was "the new girl who hadn't been here long and didn't know much."

The day went well until late in the afternoon when my sister said she started getting strange and had "that look on her face." Tonight after we came home, my mother thought she was going to die—indigestion again? The Zantac® and Mylanta® have helped for a while, but lately they don't seem to be doing so well—or perhaps the problem was leaving them off for a little while when she was so sick. I gave her Mylanta® tonight. She's terribly swelled. As soon as we got here, she wanted everything off, even her socks, and I put a cool, loose gown on her. She even wanted the door open to let in some cool air. I was afraid she would want to sit up all night waiting to die. At 7:30 p.m. I asked her if she wanted to go to bed. She said no, that it was too early and that she never went to bed this early. The opposite is true—usually I have a hard time keeping her up until 7:00 p.m. I gave her a Thoridazine® and got her dentures out and sat up with her.

We finally got to bed at 11:00 p.m. She was sweet and very cooperative, wanting to do just what I said she needed to do after going to the bathroom. Then at 2:00 a.m., she said that she could sleep so much better in her chair. I guess I can understand considering how badly she is swelled right now.

She slept soundly in her chair the rest of the night. She was in a good mood this morning at breakfast. I was even rested after sleeping on the couch the rest of the night. I'm coming to accept this is just the way it has to be. I can rest on the couch if she isn't wandering and agitated, and I think that maybe that seems to be getting a little better. So all is well, after all.

Tuesday, May 9, 1995

I can't believe we're up so early—11:00 p.m. I did sort of expect something though, because at bedtime my mother said she had a headache. I think mainly she was confused over the TV show we watched. She seemed to be enjoying "The Walton's" (CBS, 1972-1982) so much, and then a father and son were fighting, with lots of loud voices, and that look came on her face.

She didn't seem to be too confused when she got up just now. It might have been the dream, or maybe she even remembered something from the show. When I told her it was too early to get up, she said she had been "hearing them talking in there".

Over-stimulation from today might be somewhat to blame. My mother was nervous all day. She walked outside three times starting at 8:00 a.m. and went to sit on the porch swing four times.

Her swelling seems to have gone down some. She seemed to feel well and pretty cheerful all day, and she was even hungry at supper and ate almost everything on her plate. I'm thankful for days like this, even if we do have some getting up to do at night.

Wednesday, May 10, 1995

It turned out not to be an up-all-nighter after all. Where I sit on the staircase much of the time, I can see my mother's feet and tell if she is getting up. Sometimes, though, she moves them closer to her chair, and I can't see them. I thought that was what had happened last night.

But when I went to look, she wasn't there. I hadn't heard her get up at all, though I was sitting only about six feet away. I searched through the house for her and found her back in bed, less than fifteen minutes after she had gotten up.

She was up again around 1:00 a.m., looking for "U.S."—her husband, my father. I hate it when she wakes up looking for him. I don't want to tell her he's dead, but I don't want her to go on looking and worrying. This time she forgot quickly, it seemed, and she got back in bed and went to sleep.

Friday, May 12, 1995

Every time I think we're doing so much better and my mother is so good that I think I could keep on taking care of her for years and years—then we are up again at night. It's only 11:00 p.m. now, and we're up. She tried getting up a couple of hours ago. Then I guess I was successful in convincing her that this was her house, that was her bed, and she was where she was supposed to be. This time she didn't ask, and she didn't say a word—just got up and headed for her chair.

This afternoon she sent me to town for a pair of walking/work shoes since my old ones were so torn up and dirty from working in the garden. She gave me fifteen dollars to buy them. At bedtime she said she liked it better when it was just me and her and none of "the other girls" were here. I guess she thinks we switch and a different "girl" comes after bedtime.

Thursday, May 18, 1995

I haven't written here in almost a week because everything has been going along fine—actually wonderfully, considering how bad it can get at times. There has been an occasional time at night when my mother has asked her usual "What are we doing here?" and pleaded "I want to go home," but it hasn't kept her up any this week.

She has seemed ok physically except for having some diarrhea, which does upset her, making her think she's been given something that caused it. This afternoon she's been upset with me because after she came to tell me how hot she was, I opened the door and turned on the fan (there is no air conditioning in the house, except one small and very old window-unit in the kitchen). It's getting to the point that she doesn't know how to ask for what she wants (how do I know for sure if she is hot or cold?), and it sometimes seems that no matter what I do, I don't please her.

She hasn't walked outside in two days—says she just doesn't think she could make it. I wish she would try. She seems more like her old self, so much happier and more content, when she's walking outside.

Friday, May 19, 1995

We are up now at a little after 9:00 p.m., just a couple of hours after going to bed. My mother seems to be hallucinating. She said she got up "to see him" and she pointed across the room, at the TV set, I think. She got really irritated with me when I went with her to the bathroom, too.

I'm so sleepy, and I can't sit up. I'm going to see if I can get a little more rest on the couch.

Saturday, May 20, 1995

Last night went much better than I expected. We were back in bed by 11:00 p.m. When my mother woke up from sleeping in her chair, she looked like she could barely move because of the way she had been sitting—with her head bent over, almost touching her lap. I had thought I should get her to lean back in her chair, but the way she had been hallucinating and agitated, I was afraid to try. When she woke up, she thought the wrap over her legs was a baby, and she wanted to take it back to bed with her. I let her take it to bed with her—no sense in trying to tell her it's a blanket when she sees it as a baby. She slept peacefully the rest of the night with the wrap beside her.

This morning I think she has a touch of diarrhea, and she still acting a bit strange. She's seeing other people here. She didn't want to eat breakfast, but I persuaded her to eat a little. I'm out of here in two hours—for my Alzheimer's support group meeting and a day of shopping!

Sunday, May 21, 1995

It's happening in the daytime this time. We didn't go to my sister's today. This afternoon she woke up from napping in her chair and was upset because she thought she saw someone outside cutting something—"that boy" she said, was doing something he wasn't supposed to do, something "that man" wouldn't like. When I told her there wasn't anyone out there, she really got angry and told me I was always saying that. When I said, "Then show him to me," she just started wandering though the house and getting more and more angry. I tried to calm her, to tell her everything was ok and that I was taking care of everything. She blew up again and said that I was trying to take over everything, to take everything from her. I just walked away from her for a while, far enough away that she couldn't see me but still close enough that I could watch her. When she sat down, I sat down in the next room.

She got up a few minutes later to go to the bathroom. I followed to help her, and she started asking me about what was going on. It seemed she thought I was a different person, not the one she had just been talking to. After the bathroom visit, I talked to her about trusting and not worrying for at least half an hour, and I finally got her calmed down. When I asked, she didn't know what started it all or what it was about. She had forgotten, and I told her that was what her disease does to her and why she needs to just trust people and not worry about things.

We walked outside, had a snack, and now she's resting in her chair again. I'm tired but relieved.

Monday, May 22, 1995

My mother is sleeping so much better at night, but she has been more confused in the daytime lately. She doesn't understand anything I say sometimes. She got really angry today when I asked if she needed to go to the bathroom. Then she took a nap and a few minutes later when she woke up, she was so sweet. She understood this time, and I took her to the bathroom. It was like I was a brand new person to her, yet someone she knew and loved. She said she wished I lived with her. I told her that I do, and it made her so happy that she cried. Then I asked who she thought I was, and she said "my sister".

Wednesday, May 24, 1995

I think the herbal teas are helping us both rest at night, and maybe even be a little calmer in the daytime, too. Yesterday I told my mother I was going to fix myself a nice relaxing cup of chamomile tea, and she said, "Make me one, too". Afterwards she was so relaxed and rested well in her chair.

There are still bad times, though. This morning she woke up from a dream really agitated, and she asked me why those kids were in here. I calmly told her there were no kids here as I helped her to the bathroom.

When we got back to her chair, I gave her some Mylanta® because I could hear gas in her stomach. Then I told her I was going to fix her a cup of chamomile tea like yesterday. She made no reply this time.

Thursday, May 25, 1995

It's really getting hot here, really too hot to drink hot tea. That makes bedtime difficult. My mother doesn't like me to use the fan, but we have to, with no air conditioning. It's hard for anyone to be comfortable when it's like this, so I can understand us being up tonight since 9:00 p.m.

Saturday, May 27, 1995

We didn't have a good beginning to our night last night. My mother was silent at supper and didn't seem to enjoy watching TV afterwards. It seemed she had indigestion, so I gave her something for that. It was so hot in the house, and I couldn't get it cooled down. My mother kept saying she was hot, and then that she was cold. She said she was hurting all over—her head, her stomach, and her toes. She was very swelled again.

I got her to bed, but we were there for only an hour. We sat up for an hour, had a cup of tea, and then we went back to bed and slept well the rest of the night except for one incident around midnight. When I woke up, I found her moving her bedside potty from between our two beds.

I asked her what was wrong, and she said, "He's there, on that bed" as she pointed to my bed. I told her I had just been there, sleeping on that bed, and that there was no one else here. She then got very angry and called me a liar, even after I turned the light on to show her what I had said was true. It seems she was still hallucinating, still seeing someone there in my bed, and as I went to the bathroom with her (she insisted on going in the other side of the house), she accused me of being with "that old boy", and she kept saying "I'm going to tell." I helped her back in bed and asked if she would like a blanket over her as well as the sheet, since it was cooling down. She grabbed the blanket and angrily shook it at me. Then she turned over and fell sound asleep. She woke up a couple more times during the night, when she used her bedside potty and then obediently got back into bed for more good sound sleep.

Sunday, May 28, 1995

Here we go again—another holiday when all the family is getting together, and the first time since Christmas that my mother's two granddaughters are here at the same time. After looking forward to it all week, this morning she says she's not going to the Memorial Day cookout.

But it's only 7:00 a.m. There's plenty of time. She thinks she's dying today. I've given her Zantac® with her two bites of breakfast, and just now I gave her Mylanta®. We will keep working on it and maybe try again with a little more breakfast or a snack at 9:00 a.m. Maybe after that she will be feeling better.

We had another night that wasn't so good, but yet it was better than sitting up all night. She wanted to get up several times between 8:00 p.m. and 10:00 p.m., but I encouraged her to stay in bed, thinking we would have a better day today if she did. By 10:00 p.m. she was really mad at me. When she used the bathroom, I handed her toilet paper as usual, but she didn't use it. When I tried to do it for her, she hit me all over and pushed me away from her, telling me I was "a bad old thing", and something about how I had "took over and tore up this house." Sometime I feel like this is all so beyond my abilities and I wonder why I'm here trying to take care of her. But I know I couldn't live with myself if I didn't give it a try at least.

Monday, May 29, 1995

It is 3:00 a.m. My mother tried to get up an hour ago, but she was good-natured and agreeable when I told her it was around midnight, although she did say "You always say that". Really, I thought it was around midnight. I think I had been lying there awake most of the time since around 11:00 p.m. when she had gotten up to use the bathroom.

A few minutes ago she was seeing a man in the bedroom, or rather in the small bathroom that adjoins the bedroom. When I turned the light on in the bathroom to show her there was no one there, she said, "You're in danger."

I got up with her and she agreed to have a cup of chamomile tea. She told me to watch myself while fixing it, still feeling that there was some-one in the other side of the house.

It's 3:30 a.m. now. We've had our cup of tea, and when I took her to the bathroom just now, my mother asked me something about "a killer". I told her she'd just had a bad dream. When she sat back down in her chair, I thought I'd better ask her a little more about it, her dream, her hallucination, whatever it was, and it might help if we talked about it. But she was totally non-responsive, except she had a strange grin on her face. Now she was scaring me, so I retreated to the next room to wait it out.

As for yesterday—Memorial Day—all went well. She woke up, agreeing to take a bath. She fell back asleep, and I was afraid she would not be so agreeable when she woke again. I was right. She was complaining about having to be with people today, so I reminded her that those people were the ones who loved her most and the ones who she loved. She was fine all day except for getting tired in the afternoon.

It's 8:00 a.m. now. This morning has still been strange, even after day-light. At 4:30 a.m., I got so sleepy and lay down on the couch. By 4:45 a.m. my mother had woke up. I went to the bathroom with her and then talked her into going back to bed for an hour. She stayed for almost an hour, and when she got up she seemed fine at first. But then she said she couldn't find hers, that it had her name on it. I asked what she was looking for, and she replied that she didn't know. Then again during breakfast, she wanted to know where was hers, it had her name on it, everybody's had their names on them, I just wasn't doing it right, and why wasn't I feeding the others breakfast?

She kept talking this way, even though she ate most of her breakfast, took her pills, and let me help her get dressed. While I was washing dishes, I noticed she kept staring at me from where she sat in her chair. Once she got up and came to me, asking why didn't Myrtle Lee (my sister) send for her. I assumed that she had forgotten about the cookout we'd had yesterday and thought it was to happen today. But trying to explain does no good on days like today. Over and over she asks why this, why that, this is broke, that is dead, this is all torn up, something's just not right. She looks to me to fix things, to make them right. There's no convincing her that things are already right, that nothing is torn up, that things are as they should be—especially on days when she's not understanding anything I say, or not remembering it as soon as I've said it.

CHAPTER 9

SOLEMN SUMMER

Suspicious Eyes

You look at me with suspicious eyes,
eyes full of mistrust and anger.
You think I'm here to take away
your home, to steal your money,
to mistreat you.
You see me as different people,
all out to get you.
You think I am responsible
for this cage you are in—
this prison of confusion
called Alzheimer's.
You don't know I am doing
my best for you.
You don't even know
I am your daughter.
You stare at me from
behind suspicious eyes,
full of fear, grief, confusion.
You stare at me,
pleading for release from this prison.
I reach out to you,
not knowing whether
you will hug me or hit me.

Sunday, June 4, 1995

We've had a wonderful week except for one night when things got pretty bad and I called my sister to come try to calm my mother down and see if she could get back into bed. My mother got up hysterical, talking about someone, my brother, her brother, something about someone's brother going to kill someone. She was demanding that I call someone about it. That was about 10:00 p.m. My sister and I sat with her for about two hours, trying to convince her that nothing was wrong and that she should quit worrying and go back to bed.

Tonight she got up wanting food and is angry with me for not cooking something—she feels that she hasn't had a meal all day and that I'm making her go hungry. It is midnight. I gave her ice cream, but that hasn't satisfied her. I also made the mistake of getting her to put her dentures in (pretty dumb, since they weren't necessary for eating ice cream), and now I don't think I'll be able to get them out again. She was shaking so with anger when she was putting them in, and I was so afraid she would drop and break them.

We had such a good day today. We ate at my sister's and then when my mother fell asleep in her chair there, I came home to clean house and do some garden work. I saw them from the garden, sitting under the trees on the hill watching me. My mother seemed content and happy. I could imagine my sister was telling me how hard I was working, making the flowers in the garden spot pretty for her to enjoy.

Tonight, though, I'm afraid my mother wants to get rid of me again.

Monday, June 5, 1995

I've just turned down an opening for my mother at the nursing home in town where my sister has had her on a waiting list even before I came home, I think. They had a bed that needed to be filled today. My sister didn't pressure me, and when I said "no", she said she thought that was what I would say.

I don't know if that was a mistake. But for right now, I think it was the right thing to do. Things have been getting some better, and we've had some really good days, even some better nights, too, lately.

We were up only a few minutes longer last night. I left my mother alone and wrote in my journal, sitting in the next room. When I came back to check on her, she was cooperative. She had gotten up to walk into the kitchen, and I followed her. She was distressed by "being left here" by her mother or by Myrtle (my sister, who often in her mind is her sister, her sister-in-law as last night, or sometimes perhaps even her mother). She let me help her get her dentures out, and then she went back to bed and slept a couple of hours.

At 2:00 a.m. she was up before I realized it, on the other side of my bed, shaking me to awaken me. According to what she was saying, it sounded like she had already been into the other side of the house. She was telling me about people being in there. I turned on the lights to show her there was no one, and she pointed to the few dishes we had used just before bedtime (a couple of glasses, the cups we'd used for our chamomile tea and the bowl she'd had her ice cream in at midnight.) She said those people had used those and left dirty dishes in the sink. She started complaining about thing being messed up and needing to be cleaned (except for those few dishes and the area where I sit on the staircase in the next room, the house was spotless because I had just cleaned it that day). Then she started talking about "that boy" who she said was in bed with me, so I took her back to the bedroom and showed her there was no one there.

I may be crazy, but I can't let her go yet. My life is too wrapped up in caring for her and doing all I can to try to make life a little more comfortable and cheerful for her. How can I let her go when she is my life?

Wednesday, June 14, 1995

I haven't written here in a week and a half because I haven't felt the need so much. My mother has her moments of extreme confusion; times of seeming stubbornness when I could almost regret my decision about the nursing home, but things have been so much better. There have been no long nights of sitting up with her. The closest we've been to that lately was last night when she couldn't go to sleep when we first went to bed, so we got up for another hour of TV and chamomile tea.

She is so much calmer lately. Even if she does have a bit of a catastrophic reaction in the night in response to a dream or hallucination, she's usually back in bed just a few minutes later, as she was last night, carrying her leg wrap ("the baby") with her. She had been angry because she thought I was mistreating "the babies"—she had said that as she pointed to the bed covers.

This is something that occurs pretty often. She thinks I'm mistreating babies, children, or old people that she thinks are here in the house with us. Last night was one of the "I'm going to tell Myrtle" nights—meaning that she was going to tell my sister that she didn't want me here with her anymore. I'm getting used to that, though.

Friday, June 23, 1995

Again, things have been going along so well that I haven't felt the need to write here, until today. Now it's really bad. I'm glad tomorrow is my shopping trip/Alzheimer's support group meeting day, so that I can get away from here for one day.

Yesterday morning at snack time my mother had indigestion that we couldn't seem to get rid of. Right in the middle of it, the Home Health nurse came to re-take a blood test—because of too high potassium levels. This has happened before, and just seemed to have been because the blood sat too long after they got it before it went to the lab.

To top things off, I had to have my mother ready for a 3:00 p.m. neurologist appointment without letting her know until after lunch—for fear of a negative reaction.

The doctor's trip went surprisingly well, but afterwards didn't. My mother was so tired, didn't want to watch TV after supper, didn't want to go to bed either after her pills, grabbed her dentures away from me when I was trying to put them in the container to soak for the night, making me spill water on her. Her dress got wet, and she complained, but she fought me as I was trying to help her out of the wet dress and into her nightgown. She slapped me and told me she wanted me to get out of here and never come back.

I called my sister, because my mother was so hysterical, and I thought maybe her talking to her would get her calmed down. It did, and she got her into bed. In a few minutes, though, my mother was back up.

But she was all smiles, telling me very sweetly that she would like supper, that she didn't get any (I had to coax her into eating any supper at all earlier). As she ate a snack, the smiles went away—I guess she remembered something, and she was apologetic.

Though my mother was all right for the rest of the night last night, she has been silent today. She has turned down walking outside on a beautiful day. When I asked if she wanted to talk or if she wanted me to read to her, she said she just wanted to be left alone.

Saturday, July 8, 1995

I haven't written here in over two weeks. It isn't because there haven't been incidents I could write about, little things I've observed about my mother, both perplexing and amusing. But there have been no more nights of her getting up to stay up during the night and no more major catastrophic reactions. She occasionally wakes up during the night confused, but if I can get her to use the bathroom, then she will crawl right back into bed.

The Fourth of July didn't go well at first, but we found a solution. We were at my sister's, and my mother didn't want to go out to the backyard to eat with the family after waking up from a nap in a recliner. We wouldn't give in and made her go out, telling her everyone was out there and wanted to be with her because they loved her. She was a little better after eating some. Then a niece brought her a puppy to hold, and she seemed more content than I think I've ever seen her, just sitting holding a little collie puppy all afternoon.

I am fortunate to have these memories of my mother—the times we walk outside, sit under the peach trees on the bench looking at the flower bed I've fixed for her (now abloom with impatients, with coleus, and caladiums sprinkled throughout them), the times I read to her, or when we sit holding hands watching a good movie. This is the year of my life—the year when I'm doing something really worthwhile and saving memories to last a lifetime. I hope that there will be at least one more year of this.

Monday, July 10, 1995

We had a setback last night. My mother began trying to get up at 10:00 p.m. Each time I told her it was still night, she got angrier. She said she wished I had never come here. One time she told me I had been "saying it was night all day." She was up continually between 3:00 a.m. and 5:00 a.m.—wandering through the house, stumbling and almost falling, but refusing my offers for help. She did go back to bed each time, but only after wandering throughout the house. I got no sleep, because as soon as we went back to bed, she was up again. Then when she got up at 5:00 a.m., she asked why she had been "left in this place." I told her it was her home, told her all about herself and her family, as I have done hundreds of times before.

Breakfast and the rest of the morning have gone fine. She is taking a nap in her chair now.

Thursday, July 13, 1995

I don't know why last night—or rather 2:00 a.m. this morning—hurt so much more than usual. I don't know if it was what my mother said or just how she said them or what she did. Maybe I was just tired and it hurt more this time. She said the same things she's said before: That she wishes I had never come, that I was trying to take over everything and to take her house from her, and that I didn't fix her anything to eat all day yesterday. She sat on the side of the bed and told me that she wanted me to leave her alone and that when daylight came she was telling someone in her family that she was getting me out of here.

She had crawled back in bed by 3:00 a.m., and she slept until 6:00 a.m., but I didn't sleep much. I lay there and cried for over an hour.

I fixed her an extra special breakfast this morning, but she didn't eat it. She had jerked away from me at 6:00 a.m. when I tried to help her put her robe on, and she was still angry with me at breakfast.

Friday, July 14, 1995

We are up at 10:30 p.m. tonight, just three hours after going to bed. My mother said it was too hot in the bedroom. Actually it was cooling a lot in the bedroom because of the fans in there, but it's as hot as can be here in the other side of the house.

It is getting worse again, and I don't know how much longer I can do it. I thought I could make my mother happy by coming home to take care of her, but I'm not. Maybe a nursing home would be better for her.

Tuesday, July 18, 1995

I don't know what is happening this month. We're having really bad times every couple of days. One of them was around 6:00 p.m. on Sunday.

There was a storm. I brought my mother's supper to her at her chair so she wouldn't have to come to the kitchen. She ate it, but when I started giving her medicine, she had a little trouble getting one pill down, and she got really angry. She said she wasn't supposed to take this medicine.

I had turned the TV on after the thunderstorm ended, and we were watching a movie. Suddenly my mother yelled: "Get those kids out of here!" She started pacing the floors, and I just left her doing that after I saw my trying to explain was doing no good. I went to get the beds ready for the night. She followed after me and, thinking I was a different person, told me that I didn't know what was going on in this house and all about that woman in there trying to give her those pills.

We talked about it for a little while, and I told her I was only giving her the medicine she takes every night. She told me that she wasn't sick and that she didn't know that I was staying with her. She said that she couldn't pay me.

Finally when she was calm, we went back to watching TV, taking medicine, and then to bed, with no more problems.

But we have had problems all day yesterday and so far today until I took her for a walk, read to her, and then she fell asleep. She is either too hot or too cold (cold in July?), the food is no good (though the same food was good yesterday), there's too much noise (from my cooking and washing dishes?), or I'm mistreating the children or old folks she thinks are living here.

Thursday, July 20, 1995

Meal times usually seem to be torture for my mother. She usually pushes back her plate, eating only a fourth of what I've given her, which is only a small portion anyway. Today she ate only a few bites. I asked her today to let me know when she feels bad, and if it's indigestion, I can give her something for it before mealtime so that she will feel better and we can eat.

But we weren't communicating so well today. When I said that, she thought I was accusing her of taking something that wasn't hers. So she decided she wouldn't eat or take any medicine again, because she thinks I'm trying to kill her.

Last night we were watching an old "The Walton's" (CBS, 1972-1982) rerun. Even on her favorite TV shows, there's something occasionally that will upset her. In that episode, Cora Beth was developing a drinking problem. I brought my mother a glass of water to take a pill with, and she wouldn't touch it—she thought it was some of Cora Beth's alcohol. Same thing with the glass of diet cola in my hand—she thought I was drinking. She got hysterical, said she was never drinking any water here again, and she told me she wanted me out of her house. I had to call my sister to come try to calm her down.

CHAPTER 10

▼

SUMMER'S END

Many Faces

How can you want to hold hands with me
at night when we watch TV
when you have talked to me the way
you have during the day?
How can you hug me and tell me you love me
when you hit me just a
few hours before?
How can you be so good, so cooperative
at times, and at other times scream:
"I will not!"
What a terrible thing this is,
that makes you change so;
I never know what to expect
the many faces of Alzheimer's.

Friday, August 4, 1995

For two weeks everything has been almost perfect—except for some daytime confusing and "getting lost" right here at home. My mother has slept well every night. One night she woke only twice for going to the bathroom! But tonight is another story.

She was all worn out and wanted to go to bed at 6:00 p.m. after a day of being rather nervous and not doing much of her daytime napping. She's been trying to get up since 9:00 p.m. Every time it was a different question: "Why are we in a place like this?", "Why are all these people here?", "Why are you here?, Who invited you here?, Don't you have some other place to stay?" She was hungry, so I gave her a snack. Now at 11:30 p.m., she's sitting in her chair, wide-awake but silent, not appearing to hear or understand anything I say to her. It looks like we will be up all night.

Saturday, August 5, 1995

Thankfully, my mother went back to bed last night at midnight and went to sleep. But it took me a long time to get back to sleep. She was up again at 4:00 a.m., up and down and wandering all over the house, talking about some man wanting her money. At 5:00 a.m. she sat in her chair and I fixed breakfast.

We're up again tonight. It started the same way, with my mother wanting to go to bed as soon as my sister left from her afternoon visit, and before we'd had supper. I rushed supper up and got her there by 6:00 p.m. But she kept getting up from 7:00 p.m. to 8:00 p.m., using the bathroom and talking excitedly about some kind of plans she was making, some kind of work that had to be done that she was letting me do. At 9:30 p.m. she got up, saying "he" is here and that the work "must be done now." Now at 9:40 p.m., she's fallen asleep in her chair.

Thursday, August 17, 1995

Things have been going pretty well till the last three nights. My mother has been just sitting on the side of the bed, not getting back in bed or going anywhere else. Last night she sat there, and at midnight she told me to get out of bed and fix her something to eat.

On Tuesday night she kept sitting up, and at 1:00 a.m., I got the big wedge pillow that I bought for her and suggested she prop herself up on it, and maybe she could still go to sleep that way. I lay back down and watched her. I dozed a little as I watched, but I don't think she slept much herself from 1:00 a.m. until 3:00 a.m. Then she lay back down and slept until 7:00 a.m. We really got lucky that time!

But not this time. My mother was up and down from 11:00 p.m. until midnight when she ordered me to get up and fix her something to eat. She said, "None of ya'll don't ever fix me anything to eat."

After she ate, she calmed down. She leaned against the big wedge pillow for a couple of hours, but again, I don't think she slept much until she lay back down at 2:00 a.m. But I'm not lucky like yesterday—we're up now at 4:00 a.m.—to stay it seems.

Tuesday, September 5, 1995

Again, I haven't written in here in a while, not because there have not been any problems, but perhaps because I was too busy attempting to solve them and just too tired to write anything down. I had also lost my journal. I'm getting really bad about losing things under my piles of mail and books.

Though my mother is sleeping for longer periods of time at night usually, it still seems she is getting up more confused and wanders through the house at all hours of the night. I've found out most often all she really needs to do is to use the bathroom, but getting her there is a major task. Often she is just fine as soon as she's made the bathroom visit, and she just crawls back in bed. But until she does it, she is often hysterical.

At 3:00 a.m. this morning she wandered through the house several times, talking on and on but saying hardly anything I could understand. There was a sense of urgency, and she was upset about something she was looking for or something that had to be done. Finally I got her to go back to bed at 4:15 a.m., only to get right back up again. This time I got her to sit on her potty, though she got very angry with me. But as soon as she had used it she was calm, and she crawled back in bed and slept peacefully until 6:00 a.m.

It's getting to be this way every night lately. Always the same thing—she just needs to use the bathroom but doesn't know it. She doesn't understand what I'm saying when I tell her so. She gets angry, and her anger grows until we finally have a bathroom visit.

During the day, any little noise from the kitchen will make her angry sometimes. If I drop something, I'm really in trouble. Sometimes if I even touch her, just to help her up from her chair to go to the bathroom or to the table at mealtimes, I'm in trouble. Either my hands are too cold or I've hurt a sore place on her arm.

Sometime in the past couple of weeks I passed the one-year mark. I have been taking care of my mother for a year now. I don't know how much longer I can go on. And yet, I've invested so much into taking care of my mother, and it is my life now—I have no other life to go back to. So how can I give up now?

Sunday, September 17, 1995

I'm nearly a month into the second year with my mother, and I'm so afraid this is the end, not the beginning of another year.

My mother's confusion and her hallucinations and delusions are growing worse all the time. Just in the past two weeks, it has seemed that she's had a total break with reality—not just some of the time or much of the time, but all of the time. Not only does she not recognize any of us as her children, but also she doesn't think she has ever had children. Nor does she think she's ever been married, and she doesn't even recognize the name when her late husband, my father, is mentioned.

We used to have bad times and good times both, but now it's mostly just bad times. There's no longer a time when things are better. Her bad reactions are no longer caused by something I can figure out, because now they always seem to be reactions to her dreams, hallucinations, and delusions and to the fact that I don't know what to do about them to make things alright for her. Always there's something she thinks has to be done immediately, but usually she can't communicate well enough to let me know what needs to be done. How can I go along with what she wants or what she thinks when I don't know what it is?

Monday, September 18, 1995

It had seemed we were going to be up the rest of the night last night, but we weren't. My mother was up for only an hour from 11:00 p.m. until midnight. Finally I got her to go to the bathroom, and then she went back to bed and slept until 6:00 a.m. this morning, except for getting up three times to use her bedside potty.

This morning I had a hard time getting her to go to the bathroom. I kept asking, and she kept saying she didn't need to. I was worried that she would need to when the plumbers were here, fixing the sink, commode, and bathtub—all of which were leaking, as well as the well pump which hasn't been working since Friday night. I have had to carry water in buckets from a water hose run from my sister's house to the back yard here. We couldn't get anything done about it Saturday because my youngest niece, my sister's daughter, was getting married. All of us, except my mother, had planned to be there. Things always seem to go wrong at the very worst times around here.

Fortunately, my mother doesn't even seem to realize anything is wrong. Things went smoothly while we were at the wedding. The lady who had stayed with her before I came home was with her. I was a bundle of nerves, just thinking about all that could have gone wrong, because my mother, in her confusion, hasn't been very sweet lately. But the lady said she was good and everything went just fine. It was like my mother had an old friend visiting her, and they seemed to have a wonderful day.

My mother slept in her chair most of the morning. I did finally get her to go to the bathroom before the plumbers got here. When they got here I tried to explain to her that a few things were being fixed. That seemed to be fine with her at first, though she did jump with every noise they made, and she told me they were "walking heavy" when they came through the house. I kept her as calm as possible by showing her pictures in magazines, books, and finally some old photo albums. Still she jumped with every noise that came from the bathroom pipes and as the men walked through. I was still a bundle of nerves all day. It wasn't just everything in this old house tearing up and needing repair, but also that my mother might explode at any minute because of strange men coming into the house. When they left, she was exhausted and angry with me, and worried about how she would pay the plumbers, which I told her had been taken care of already. But she soon fell asleep and forgot.

When I talked to her once today, my mother had tears in her eyes. She was cuddled under covers in her chair, like a little girl who knows she's been bad and is truly sorry. I felt like going to her and wrapping my arms around her and telling her I'll never leave her. So I did just that, except for telling her the "I would never leave her" part. We hugged and cried together. She is smiling now. She says I'm going to help her get well.

I want so much to keep on taking care of her. We have had some good times. We've had some terrible times, but some very good times too. But when she's so confused and seeing and hearing things, I just don't know what to do anymore.

My mother is on a nursing home waiting list. I've turned down an opening for her twice since I've been home. I want to turn it down next time, too. But can I keep on going this way?

My sister says she's ready any time I am to put her in the nursing home. My brother-in-law says it would be different if I were helping to make her better, but that I'm not. She's not going to get any better, no matter how hard I try to take good care of her.

But how will she react to a nursing home? And how am I to pick up the pieces and go on with my life knowing I've put her there?

Friday, September 22, 1995

My mother has really been out of it all day. It's our second day in a row of dark cloudy days, and she's been sundowning when awake and sleeping the rest of the time. She's been so confused. I thought it might be indigestion and gave her something for it, but she still wasn't any better. The Home Health aide just gave her a sponge bath instead of trying a shower. She said two others she had seen today were out of control. My mother hasn't been out of control today, not since just before daylight, except for begging "to go home" just before the Home Health aide came, and then telling me that she could see her "daddy in a casket over there." She hardly ate dinner, and for the second or third day in a row, could not seem to remember how to swallow her pills and just held them in her mouth or chewed them up.

The way things have been lately, I'm wondering if it's a new stage of the disease and not just the weather. This morning early she just sat on the side of her bed and was angry with me for asking if she needed to use the bathroom or if she was ready to get up—she didn't want to move or go back to bed—just sat there, and well, she did hit me and told me to leave her alone.

I hope that there will be a few brighter days left. Monday I was surprised when I was showing her the old photo albums. It was like just seeing the pictures brought her back for a few minutes. She could identify old friends and family, and even some of her children. There have been other times when I've tried this, and she hasn't been able to identify anyone.

Monday, September 25, 1995

We've been up since midnight. My mother has diarrhea, but she won't let me give her anything for it. She's pretty calm though, and she just wants to sit in her chair.

In about four and a half hours I will be turning forty years old. I guess it's appropriate we sit up tonight to greet that momentous birthday. (ugh!)

Tuesday, September 26, 1995

We didn't stay up too long yesterday morning—just about an hour, and we slept till around the time I turned forty—at 5:00 a.m.

We are up now at 3:30 a.m. The weather is getting cooler again, and like before, I try to get my mother to stay in bed until I can warm up this side of the house, but I wasn't successful at that this morning.

Wednesday, September 27, 1995

Last night was much better, except when my mother got up to use the bathroom and seemed to have some diarrhea; she blamed it on her medicine and said she wasn't taking it any more.

It's now 5:30 a.m., but I'm not fixing breakfast just yet. My mother is confused, and it would be better if we can wait till daylight, so hurry sunrise!

Thursday, September 28, 1995

We were up at just past midnight for the rest of the night. My mother said she was just tired of "standing up", her words at the moment for lying down. We went to bed early though. She was so tired at 5:00 p.m., and after supper, she couldn't seem to enjoy TV at all, so I let her go to bed at 6:00 p.m., so actually we had practically a full night's sleep.

Friday, September 29, 1995

We were up earlier this time, just half an hour or so before midnight. I wonder if it's kind of a habit and that once it starts again, it continues for a while. But it's better to get up than to try to get her to stay in bed, I think—at least we avoid the anger. I'm so tired though. I thought I wasn't going to make it during the afternoon yesterday. For a little while it was like I couldn't stay awake a minute longer.

Saturday, September 30, 1995

My mother did go back to bed Thursday night about an hour later, but she was up really early again. Or was that just this morning? I can't remember anymore. Am I getting Alzheimer's already?

Last night I had my first experience of taking care of my mother while I myself was physically sick (and I still am a bit today). I started feeling sick this afternoon with heartburn and nausea. I felt so awful that I couldn't go buy groceries when my sister came to stay with my mother so I could do that. I took several antacids, but they didn't help much.

After a while, I told my sister I was better and that she didn't have to stay. I fixed chicken soup for supper for my mother and I—thought maybe I could eat that and she would enjoy it for a change. She did, and I ate most of mine, but I didn't keep it long.

I started feeling better after I threw up, and then I had a cup of tea. Today all I've had was crackers and soft drinks and just a little oatmeal at breakfast. I still feel weak and still hurt a little—my stomach and head, too.

My mother isn't doing so well either. She's acting very strangely. She slept in her chair for several hours after breakfast (which is normal), but when she woke up and I took her a snack, she didn't seem to know what to do with it—just held it in her hand. I tried to explain that it was food and that she needed to eat it, but got no response, so I finally took it away.

CHAPTER 11

▼

FALLING DOWN

I Cry

I cry for the pain you're feeling
as your mind is
tortured.
I cry for the pain I'm feeling
as you push
me away.
I cry for all who are feeling
the pain of
this disease.
I cry for all the families
torn apart by
Alzheimers.

Tuesday, October 3, 1995

What a night we had last night! It all started out with me trying to help my mother use the bathroom, her shoving me away and saying she wanted me out of here. Then she went back to bed but kept getting up.

I took her to her chair, and she just sat there saying, "Oh Lord, Oh Lord." I left her for a few minutes, and then went back to try to get her to go to the bathroom again. She was cooperative this time, and then she went back to bed, but only for a few minutes. She said there was someone in the other side of the house, hurt and lying on the floor and that I'd better help. There could be no convincing her otherwise, I knew, so I went to the other side of the house, and then came back and told her that person was fine, and was sleeping soundly. So she went back to bed, but only for two minutes this time. She then said that the house was going to burn down and everyone was going to be killed and that it was going to be my fault if I didn't do something. We went on this way for at least an hour, or was it two? It seemed it wasn't going to end this time and I couldn't get her calmed down. So I called my sister at around 1:00 a.m., getting her and her husband out of bed, and I shouldn't have done that, not when they have to work today. I must not do this again. Every time I do this it just proves I'm not handling things well. I've got to not call them again. I've got to prove I can handle it.

Friday, October 6, 1995

It seems that everything that could go wrong has done just that in the year that I've been here with my mother. The well has run out of water several times; the pump quit working and we had to get a new one; the wiring is so bad in this house and it's always blowing something (It was wired at least fifty years ago by my father, and it wasn't wired enough for a house of this size for today's appliances); we've had leaks everywhere, commode not working; there was a wreck across the highway a month or so ago that downed power lines, including the one connected to the house, (thankfully, my mother slept through that night); and now Hurricane Opal. We've been out of electricity and water for two days so far. Trees are down in the yard and the garden, including the peach tree by the bench that was surrounded by the flowers that did so well. Now the tree is lying over the bench, the flowers are toppled, and they won't last long anyway now, no longer shaded from the sun.

My mother slept through Opal (which still had hurricane strength winds when it came through this part of Alabama) and didn't even make any comments when she got up to use the bathroom during it, while the winds were still howling wildly. She hasn't seemed to be bothered too much so far by no lights or running water, or by the cold food (sandwiches and pork-n-beans) I've served her.

But in the last few weeks it has seemed there has been a steady decline in her few remaining abilities. She can't seem to swallow pills anymore. It began gradually, but now it's just about every pill. She holds it in her mouth until it melts, or she chews it, and if it's given with food, then she says the food tastes awful, when what she actually tastes is the pill. More and more often when I bring her a snack she just holds it, as if she doesn't know what to do with it.

Yesterday at supper time my mother got upset, said she was hurting and wanted to go to bed and die. I felt she had indigestion, so I got her something for it, but she refused and said I was trying to kill her. She said she wished she had somebody good, somebody with some sense to take care of her. My sister came, and she got her to take the medicine and to eat.

If my father were still alive he would have been 94 years old today. I'm glad, for his sake, that he did not live to see my mother as she is now. He would have felt that it was his duty to care for her till the end, and I'm afraid she would have been awful to him. If she remembered him at all, it would be the young "U.S." that she married and not this old man.

It's good that he went ten years ago and it was she who took care of him during his brief period of suffering with cancer. Even back then, we know now, she had Alzheimer's, but none of us realized it. We knew she had lost her ability to do math, her writing was going, and her memory had been going gradually for years, but we all said "She's just getting older."

Sunday, October 8, 1995

We made it through our period of no electricity. The lights came back on yesterday about 6:00 p.m. My mother was fine through it all. It seemed she had only begun to worry a little today about why there was no electricity and water.

Then last night she began trying to get up at 11:00 p.m. I convinced her to go back to bed every time until 1:00 a.m. when I was no longer successful. When she got up then she said she was going to cook some breakfast because she hadn't had anything to eat. By the time I got her to her chair, got her dentures ready for her and brought a snack, she said she wasn't hungry and that she didn't want anything. She started asking for other people: my dad and other people I've never even heard of—I think she makes up names sometimes, or maybe she has someone in mind but just can't remember the name.

I was too sleepy to sit up, maybe just too worn out from the days when there was no electricity and worrying that it would begin to bother my mother. So I made myself a bed on the floor in the next room so that I could catch a nap or two and still watch her.

Thursday, October 12, 1995

The past couple of nights, we've been getting up around 1:00 a.m. to 3:00 a.m. and sitting up for a couple of hours. Tonight it was 11:00 p.m., after being in bed less than four hours.

I think that the chamomile tea and the herbal remedies I tried for helping calm my mother and helping her sleep may have worked some for two or three months (or perhaps it was the fact that we had nice weather, and were able to have some wonderful times outside in the daytime), but now they just are not working anymore.

Monday, October 16, 1995

Last night was very close to being the worst night we've ever had. My mother wandered back and forth between the bedroom and the living room a dozen times. She would say she was going back to bed, but then she didn't want to when we got there. She said that I had something ready for her and that I should give it to her. I told her I had the bed ready for her, but she didn't want to go to bed when we got there. I asked her if she needed something to eat or medicine if she was hurting, and she said no, that she didn't want either, but she did say, "I hurt all the time." She couldn't tell me what it was she wanted, but just kept wandering back and forth through all the rooms, looking for it.

Finally I got her to sit in her chair by saying, "Sit right here and tell me again what it is you want." It sounded like "bed", but there was something else I couldn't make out. All of this happened around between 1:00 a.m. and 2:30 a.m.

Earlier, before midnight, she needed to use the bathroom but I couldn't get her to use her bedside potty. She wanted to pick it up to "fix it". I had to keep trying to explain what it was for and what she needed to do. Finally she did, but only after asking, "It won't hurt her?"

The day went great yesterday for Sunday dinner at my sister's. My mother ate well at all meals yesterday, though for the three previous days she had eaten hardly anything. I was hoping we would have a better night last night after she had eaten well, but it didn't work out that way this time.

Thursday, October 19, 1995

Getting up at night is becoming a regular occurrence. So is morning and afternoon (and sometimes all day) confusion. So is refusing to eat.

The past couple of days I have called my sister-in-law to help me get my mother to take Ensure® after trying unsuccessfully to get to her to eat and to take her medicine.

She has eaten so far today, but she has been terribly confused this afternoon. She has been wandering all over the house looking for "that boy" and sometimes for "that girl" who it seems she thinks has been misbehaving.

I did something rash yesterday. When she was refusing to eat and telling me to "get out of the house!" yesterday, I called the local nursing home and told them we're ready next time they have an opening. Today I've felt I was wrong to do that, but then this afternoon has been so bad, and maybe it would be best for her too—maybe I really should let her go.

But I still don't want to. After it's over, where do I go, and what do I do, and how do I live after doing that to her?

Friday, October 27, 1995

Last night was probably the worst night we've ever had after what was probably also the worst day we've ever had. My mother was up at 8:00 p.m., before I had a chance to get to sleep, and I couldn't get her to use her potty. Finally by 9:00 p.m. she sat in her chair, and she felt asleep.

She woke up and went to the bathroom a couple of times, but when she got there, it was like she didn't know what to do and wouldn't use it. She went back to bed at 1:00 a.m., but by 2:00 a.m., she was up again, sitting on the side of her bed mumbling something I couldn't understand. I tried for a half-hour to get her to use her potty with no success. Finally she went back to bed again, only to be up again couple of minutes later. After a while I got her to walk with me to the bathroom in the other side of the house. She finally used it, but she didn't go back to bed. She was finally relaxed, though, and she was sleeping soundly in her chair by 3:30 a.m.

After going to the bathroom she had told me, "Everything will be alright now if you will just do right and leave my children and my husband alone." When I asked her if she wanted something to drink, she said no, and that all she wanted was her husband.

All that was only half of this "36-hour day" I've had.

My mother slept most of the morning, straight through her snack time. I got her to the bathroom just in time at 11:00 a.m. I thought I had better give her some Mylanta® so that hopefully there would be no problems with indigestion at lunchtime. I wasn't successful. She knocked the spoon out of my hands, spilling the medicine. A little later, I tried a cup of tea, and she hit at me, nearly knocking the cup of tea out of my hands.

I left her alone for a while. Finally I tried to get her to the table to eat lunch. She went, but wouldn't eat. She kept talking about "that boy" being "in trouble" and even something about "killing". Obviously she had been hallucinating earlier. I think she does that much of the time lately.

I finally got her to drink a can of Ensure®, but she didn't eat lunch. She had eaten only half of her breakfast this morning. Again in the evening, she ate only half of her supper, and she had eaten only half of a snack in the afternoon.

Again, she slept most of the time in the afternoon, but somehow we did manage to take a couple of walks, one just after lunch and another just before supper. I had hoped that would bring her out of so much confusion and that she would sleep better tonight.

No such luck. She was so sleepy at 6:00 p.m. that she wanted to go to bed then. She slept only until 8:00 p.m.

Saturday, October 28, 1995

We sat up from 8:00 p.m. last night until 1:00 a.m. this morning, and then went back to bed, only to be up again at 2:00 a.m. At that point, I'd had about half an hour of sleep, and only about three hours the previous night.

On the video I watched that I had borrowed from my Alzheimer's support group, a woman said she didn't sleep for three years when she was taking care of her husband.

At 5:00 a.m. this morning, my mother decided to go back to bed after going to the bathroom. She slept until 7:00 a.m., so I got two and a half hours of sleep all night, for which I am grateful, for I thought I wasn't going to have more than half an hour all night.

This morning has been fine, though it's been a cloudy day, and that never helps. The Home Health aide was able to get my mother to take a bath before the electricity went off today (again!). We will have a cold lunch. I'm glad I stocked up on things we could have for cold lunches during our Hurricane Opal experience.

Tuesday, October 31, 1995

It's Halloween night. We are sitting up just a couple of hours after going to bed. It would be convenient for trick-or-treaters, but there haven't been many here in years—too far out in the country, I guess.

The way it started tonight was that my mother got up, needing to use the bathroom, but again, not realizing that she did, and got angry with me when I tried to get her to. She told me that I was hateful when I asked her to use the potty and said she could not go back to bed. So I turned the heaters on in the other side of the house and got her robe and house shoes for her. When we got to her chair, she said she didn't want to be here, that she wanted to go back to bed. So we went back, and once there, she said she didn't want to be there either. She's sitting wide-awake in her chair now.

We had some bad times last night, too. The first time was around 11:00 p.m. I didn't hear her getting up, and when I did hear her in the next room, I found she had an accident—bowel incontinence.

Around 3:00 a.m. she was incontinent again—just urinary inconti-
nence this time, though. Each time after being cleaned up, she went back
to bed and slept well. She slept till around 6:00 a.m. this morning.

If all of this weren't enough, I'm also sick with a cold. I've had it since
Sunday, and now I'm wondering if I'm ever going to get well, because I'm
not getting much rest. This is the second time I've been sick this month.

CHAPTER 12

▼

NEARING THE END

I Could Think

I could think about
the good things:
our walks in the yard,
and kittens and flowers,
so I won't cry so hard.
I will think of these
and treasure the good
times we've had—
Through all the seasons
and all the years,
and maybe someday
I can smile through
my tears.

Wednesday, November 1, 1995

I got lucky again. We went back to bed at about 9:30 p.m. last night. But we were back up again at 2:30 a.m. I think it was my fault though. I was so sound asleep and didn't hear my mother when she got up. She used her potty, and since I wasn't awake to help her, she got up and went to her chair instead of going back to bed.

The house was so cold then. It's a wonder we both don't have pneumonia. Feels like I'm close to it with this cold I have.

I tried lying down in the next room to watch her as I dozed a little, but as soon as I did, she was up. I took her to the bathroom successfully but she was confused and didn't want to go back to bed. She went back to her chair, but I couldn't keep her covered up. She kept throwing her leg wrap off.

We did go back to bed at 4:00 a.m., but for no longer than five minutes. She was right back up again, sitting on the side of the bed. So I got her robe and shoes on her again and took her to her chair.

At about 4:30 a.m., she started talking to the sofa across the room, asking it who was going to bring breakfast. I told her it wasn't quite breakfast time, feeling that she wouldn't eat it if I fixed it so early. I could tell she wasn't understanding, so I went ahead and fixed breakfast. I got it ready, and she came to the table and ate like she was starved. I guess she was because she wouldn't eat any supper last night, so all she had was Ensure®. She didn't eat much breakfast or lunch yesterday, either.

Monday, November 5, 1995

At 10:45 p.m. tonight I sunk into my bed and pulled up the covers, thinking how nice it felt. Fifteen minutes later my mother was up. I explained to her that it was the middle of the night and that she needed to stay in bed. She went back, but was right up again. We went through the explanation again, and then again she was right back up. So I got her into her robe and house shoes and took her to her chair. She complained all the way about something (Again, I couldn't understand her). If only I could figure out what she really wants on these awful crazy nights. Lately she often can't find the words. The words and phrases she says are meaningless. Somewhere scattered among them are "She said" or "He said"—which must be coming from her dreams.

I'm so tired. And yet I don't want to give up. We had a good evening. At supper she ate well for the first time today, and she enjoyed the movie we watched tonight. I don't want to give up times like that, but I'm just so tired of being up so much at night.

Tuesday, November 6, 1995

We went back to bed for a few minutes. My mother said she wanted to. But then she was back out of bed twice. I insisted that she go back to bed each time. She finally did, but she cried herself to sleep.

A little while later she got up to use the bathroom. She went back to bed, in a good mood now, and said that it was "a good warm place". But then a few minutes later, she was up again, laughing this time. She laughed when I got her into her robe and house shoes, laughed when I told her it was midnight, and laughed as I took her to her chair.

Saturday, November 11, 1995

What a night! I feel like I haven't slept a wink. I haven't much. Here's the way it was:

6:00 p.m.-My mother began throwing up as she was having her evening tea after supper.

7:00 p.m.-All seemed well. My mother was in bed asleep.

9:00 p.m.-Confusion. My mother wouldn't use the potty. She fought me when I was trying to explain and help her.

11:00 p.m.-My mother got up again and we sat up until midnight.

1:00 a.m.-She was standing up before I got myself awake. She had been incontinent. She refused to let me change her gown and went to the other side of the house. I called my sister.

2:00 a.m.-My mother was back in bed, asleep, after fighting both my sister and I as we got her into a dry gown.

4:30 a.m.-After using her potty, my mother refused to go back to bed. She fought me when I started putting her robe and house shoes on her, and again when I covered her legs with her wrap.

Now at 5:00 a.m., she's sitting here in her chair, wrap thrown off, just staring into space. There's a slight storm going on. It has been very windy and raining hard all night, which could have had something to do with her not sleeping well. Having an upset stomach, I'm sure, didn't help either.

Friday, November 17, 1995

It's 6:00 p.m. now. My mother didn't eat supper. I can't get her to take her medicine. I can't get her dentures out or get her ready for bed. She's not going to bed. She just wants to sit up and sleep in her chair.

Tuesday, November 21, 1995

On Friday, I knew I couldn't sit up all night with my mother and still go on my shopping trip and to my support group meeting the next day. So I called my sister. She had our mother in bed by 7:00 p.m., and the rest of the night went fine.

In fact, every night has been fine since then, until this one. This one hasn't gone well at all. It's 2:00 a.m. now. It was another night of her needing to use the bathroom but not realizing it and getting angry and hitting me when I tried to show her what she needed to do. She told me that she didn't want to be with me, and that she didn't like me. The other night she told my sister that I'm just mean and she didn't want to live with me, and yes, she did want to go to a nursing home.

My sister said, "Well then, that's where you will be going." I guess I'm ready this time, myself. I don't want to, but I guess it's time now and I have to do it.

Friday, November 24, 1995

We made it through Thanksgiving Day yesterday, although I didn't think at first that my mother was going to go to my sister's at all. She told me "No!", but along with that she mumbled something about "That old boy!"

So I called my sister. My mother heard me tell her we weren't coming for Thanksgiving dinner. She sat in her chair for about a half-hour. When I saw her getting up, I went to see if she needed to use the bathroom. She said no. Then I asked her if she was ready to go to Myrtle Lee's for Thanksgiving Dinner, she nodded yes and asked, "Who said I wasn't going? I always go to everything at Myrtle's."

The day went fine except for some indigestion she had after dinner. It went really well when my niece's little dog was lying in her lap. After supper, I got us packed up and ready to come back as soon as possible, because I could see she was getting tired and restless.

When we got back, she wasn't interested in watching TV, and she wanted to go to bed at 6:00 p.m. We were up at 2:00 a.m., but that's understandable after going to bed so early. This time she has already had a full eight hours of sleep. I haven't quite, though, because whenever I'm up with her using the bathroom, it takes me a while to get back to sleep.

At 2:00 a.m. this morning she was thinking "that man" was here. When I showed her it was still dark outside and no one was coming, she said, "Well, I'll declare," but she's not going back to bed. She's convinced someone is coming.

I was lucky again, though. An hour later, she went back to bed. As she got into bed, I was afraid she wouldn't stay, because she kept talking about something needing to be done. She did stay, though, until daylight! What a wonderful feeling to be still in bed when the sun comes up!

Breakfast brought problems again. My mother was angry with me at breakfast because I wasn't feeding "the others". She said this as she pointed to the living room. So I took my breakfast to the couch and left it there. I came back to be with her as she ate breakfast, and then she got upset with me because I wasn't eating. So I went and got my breakfast back. And again, she was angry with me for not feeding the others.

I didn't get her to take her medicine. I thought I had got her to take the coated aspirin she's required to take each day. But I found it in the bottom of her juice glass. I tried later to give her one and thought she got it down that time, but a half-hour later I heard something being thrown across the floor, and sure enough, it was her pill.

My sister said I could stop trying with that and the vitamins if she won't take them on the first try (she's supposed to take a Vitamin E each day, too), but I want to at least try a few times. When she goes to the nursing home, though, it will be out of my hands, and I don't know if she will get them then.

The nursing home was the main topic of discussion yesterday with my sister, sister-in-law, a niece, and me. My sister is going to the local nursing home to see if she can speed up getting my mother in. Of course, if there's no opening, there's nothing that can be done.

I want to keep my mother through the holidays—till after Christmas and New Year's. But, as I am told, the family get-togethers only seem to confuse my mother more and get her more agitated. They don't mean anything to her any more, and most of the time she doesn't recognize any of my family anymore—at least not as who they are. My sister Myrtle Lee is her dead sister Myrtle, and my brother William is her dead brother Bill, when she does happen to recognize them as someone she knows.

It might be best for her to be in a nursing home. Maybe they can figure out how to get her to take her medicine and to eat better. Maybe they can figure out what to do about the indigestion and the swelling. Maybe she's to the point where going won't bother her, because she doesn't know any of us and doesn't believe she's at home anyway.

But what am I to do afterward? How am I to live in this house where everything will remind me my mother? Even the flowers will remind me of her, because I planted them for her. Those that come up in the spring will seem a mockery if she never gets to see them. There are more I had ordered that need to be planted, but why bother? I know I will not want to see flowers again, or hear music like we've listened to, or watch the movies we've watched. Even the singing of the birds will remind me of her, and our little stray cat, Pansy, will bring back the memories. I wish I could just win a million dollars from one of those sweepstakes so I wouldn't have to work and I could just travel and go far away and stay away for a long, long time.

Saturday, November 25, 1995

We were up last night at 10:00 p.m. and sat up until 2:00 a.m. I'd had difficulty going to sleep, and I think I had just fallen asleep before we got up at 10:00 p.m. When we did go back to bed at 2:00 a.m., I still couldn't get to sleep. Around 3:30 a.m. this morning, my mother was sitting on the side of the bed saying, "Please give me a place to lie down." I told her this was her bed and that she should lie down and go to sleep. She did, but as she was lying down, she said, "Please give me a home. This was mine. It was given to me…" I couldn't understand the rest, but I'm sure it was something about her home having been taken away from her.

Sunday, November 26, 1995

We were up again, same time last night—10:00 p.m. This time I was extremely tired and did get some sleep—about three hours.

My mother fell asleep last night softly talking to herself—nothing I could understand, though.

Yesterday afternoon she got hysterical while my sister was here, and I'm so glad she was here, because I'm just so tired lately. My sister has begun staying after her afternoon visit and through supper to try to get my mother to eat something and take her medicine, and that really has been helping.

Thursday, November 30, 1995

The end has come. It will be either tomorrow, or in the next few days, or just after Christmas. I will be pushing for the latter.

I had begun to relax the last couple of days because there were no openings in the local nursing home and no promises for getting my mother in because there were several people ahead of her on the list.

Then my sister-in-law found out there is an opening in the nursing home where she has just started working—about twenty miles south of here. It's supposed to be a fantastic nursing home, really impressive, the way my sister-in-law describes it.

So someone from there came today to talk to my mother and me. She arrived at the same time as the Home Health nurse, and she didn't stay long, because she found out most of what she need to know by watching my mother while the nurse talked to her.

So now I just hope we can hold off till after Christmas. I need three weeks to get myself ready, to get adjusted to the idea, and maybe even some plans for job-hunting. I wouldn't be able to find a job now, so close to Christmas, so I might as well remain taking care of my mother until afterwards and go ahead with our family get-together as planned.

Chapter 13

▼

The Last Christmas

Parting Thoughts

I didn't fix things
by being here,
and none of my trying
brought you much cheer.
The flowers I planted
will be a mockery
if they bloom again
without you to see.
There'll be no more Christmas—
no holidays again—
for you were everything
in my Christmas plans.
I feel a cold chill
all the way to my soul,
but Mama, please know,
that I love you so.

Friday, December 1, 1995

We had a bad night again last night. After going to bed, my mother got up every ten minutes or so, sitting on the side of her bed and talking, but saying nothing I could understand. She seemed to be in pain, so I got her something for indigestion. Then I got the big wedge pillow to see if she could try leaning against it to sleep. But she didn't. She kept sitting upright and talking, complaining about something. I couldn't get her to go to the bathroom, and if I got close to her, she would hit at me. Finally around 9:30 p.m., I got her to go the bathroom. Then she went to sit in her chair for the rest of the night.

I called my sister before I went to bed, and she agreed to let me have three more weeks with my mother. The nursing home hasn't officially approved it all yet, but they probably will in the next few days. I can go through whatever happens with my mother in the next few weeks just to have her with me that much longer and for us all to be together for one last Christmas. I don't think I could bear putting her in a nursing home just before Christmas.

Saturday, December 2, 1995

We were up just three hours after going to bed, with my mother hitting at me and pulling my hair. I couldn't get her to understand that she needed to use the bathroom. So she went to her chair, and she got me to understand that we would be sitting up the rest of the night.

That's ok. I don't have much longer to be with her, so I will take the remaining time however it comes.

Monday, December 4, 1995

We were up at 1:00 a.m. this morning. The night before, it was at midnight.

We have my mother's appointment with the nursing home's doctor today. The nursing home has accepted her. I'm not sure yet whether they mean for after Christmas or sooner. The others in the family seem to think we should go ahead and get it over with. But I just can't.

I don't want to put her in the nursing home, period. I've got nothing better to do than to take care of her. But I have lost fifteen pounds and am looking old and tired. I am so very tired and I can feel myself running low on patience with her. This is why I must let her go.

Without asking much at all the day she came, the person from the nursing home who had visited here told my sister-in-law that my mother was "in bad shape".

I think I realized that more than ever on Friday when she didn't recognize my brother Bob after she had been asking about him and wanting him to come. She even fell asleep when he was here. Before she had always seemed to know him even when she didn't know anyone else.

Tuesday, December 5, 1995

As I feared, with the over-stimulation in the afternoon from a doctor's visit, my mother would stay in bed for only an hour last night. She was nervous before going to bed, and still was when she got up an hour later. She seemed to be in a good mood, though. She sat in her chair and patted her foot, and seemed to be happy, but just didn't want to be in bed.

The day yesterday went pretty well with no major problems. The only problems at all were before the doctor's visit, and then just a little afterwards, because she was so tired when she got home.

My sister and I were impressed with the doctor who will be looking out for our mother in the nursing home. He seems like someone who will really take time for his patients and who cares about them.

Something funny happened when we were there. We saw a lady who was nearly my sister's age and they had known each other in high school. My sister is fifty-nine, and that lady is fifty-four. She asked my age, as if I was around the same age and in high school at the same time. I've only just turned forty, but I'm graying fast, have lost fifteen pounds, and I'm beginning to wrinkle. Funny, everyone used to think I looked so much younger than I really was.

Wednesday, December 6, 1995

We were up again at 1:30 a.m. It really is every night lately. The night before last, though, we were up for only an hour at 7:00 p.m. My mother tried to get up about 11:00 p.m. and 1:00 a.m., but somehow I talked her out of it. I told her we couldn't do anything about what she was talking about at night, but we would take care of it all when daylight came.

Again last night, she wouldn't use the potty when she got up, though I knew she needed too. Sometimes lately she won't do it when I take her to the bathroom during the daytime either. When she gets there she doesn't seem to know what she's there for, and doesn't seem to understand when I tell her either. She just talks about other things and responds to me as if I'm talking about something completely different. At times, it's like there's no ability to communicate at all.

Last night we had a really good evening just before bedtime. It made me wish we hadn't made this nursing home decision. My mother was more like she used to be. After eating well at supper and taking her medicine, she and I enjoyed an hour of a good movie with her holding my hand as she used to. She even told me she loved me, and she gave me a great big hug just before she crawled into bed.

Then a few hours later, though she wasn't hitting at me this time, she did get very angry with me when I tried to get her to use her potty. She did go back to bed around 2:30 a.m., but she was up again at 4:30 a.m.—same thing—potty trouble again.

Something different this time, though—she tried to get me to do it instead. It was the same thing again when I tried to get her to go to bed; She tried to get me to crawl in her bed. I told her, no, that she had to do it first, but she kept on trying to get me to, as if she were the one taking care of me. Sometimes she does that, and sometimes she's trying to get some invisible person to do something. Sometimes when we go to the bathroom, she thinks she's taking a child, it seems. A few times when she's been eating, she has poured a little milk on herself, saying she was "giving it to the baby."

Thursday, December 7, 1995

I thought we were going to make it through the night without getting up to stay last night. My mother had been getting up a lot to use the bathroom, but she had been going right back to bed. Then the last time, at 2:00 a.m., she got right back up.

But that's all right. Assuming we put her in the nursing home the day after Christmas, I have less than three weeks with my mother. Anything she does is ok.

Friday, December 8, 1995

My mother got up at 9:30 p.m. last night. For an hour before that, she had been getting up and sitting on the side of the bed. She would lie down and then get right back up again. After sitting in her chair from 9:30 p.m. until midnight, she got hysterical about something, said something about me being mean to someone, and insisted I call my sister. As my sister was coming in the door, my mother told me that she didn't want to live in my house anymore and that the reason she wanted me to call "them" was so they could take her home, and she said "I'm not staying here all night." When my sister got here, all she could say was "That crazy woman!", meaning me, I guess. My sister listened to her and somehow got her calmed down and back in bed, but not without problems. On the way to the bedroom, I guess for a minute she thought my sister was me, and she told her "Get out of my house!"

After that, she was fine and slept until 3:00 a.m. when we had a potty problem, and she got hitting angry when I was trying to help her, and again afterwards when I tried to help her cover up in bed.

Saturday, December 9, 1995

We were up at 1:30 a.m. this morning to sit up the rest of the night. My mother was calm, though, and it was fine with me to sit up. Lately I can't sleep well anyway, and I might as well be sitting up. I can write about my feelings and sort them out and maybe prepare for what is going to happen.

I was so afraid that when I called my sister at midnight Thursday night she might say, "This is it", and insist we go ahead and put our mother in the nursing home now. But she said, "The decision is still yours", and "It's still ok to hold off until after Christmas."

I wish I hadn't made the decision at all. I'm so scared of how going to the nursing home will affect her. Even at the grocery store yesterday, the boy who loaded my bags of groceries into the car shook his head and said "They go down after you put them in the nursing home. I don't know what it is, but they go down." I thought, "Thanks a lot. I really needed to hear that now the decision has been made and I can't go back on it. How I wish I could go back on it now."

Monday, December 11, 1995

We've managed to stay in bed one night (Saturday night) until just before 5:00 a.m. Then my mother woke up really confused, though we did make it through breakfast ok, but she kept talking about being afraid of something here and she wanted to be out of this house. So I thought this was a good time to take her to my sister's, and I called, asking if I could bring her extra early for Sunday dinner. My sister said to just give her time to get dressed and then bring her on. That was wonderful for me. I needed to make some phone calls, talk to some friends I'd neglected while taking care of my mother, because it's been just about impossible to continue to call and keep in touch. I needed to talk to them about what we're going to do—put my mother in the nursing home. Maybe I just needed someone to tell me I wasn't doing the most awful thing in the world. And they did. They assured me that it would probably be best for her, and that I had already done my best.

We were up at 2:00 a.m. this morning to sit up the rest of the night, but that was all right. I still needed to do some thinking, and I don't think I could have slept anyway. I stay awake and toss and turn long after we go to bed each night lately.

I'm so scared. Changes affect my mother. Just my moving in with her last year, I think, threw her into a more advanced stage of Alzheimer's, because she didn't start her night wandering and sitting up at night until then. How will going into a nursing home (even if it is such a wonderful one as my sister-in-law says) with a lot of strange people affect her? It scares me so to think of what it might do to her.

Tuesday, December 12, 1995

We were up last night at 11:30 p.m. until around 1:30 a.m. this morning. My mother was upset with me when I was helping her with using the bathroom. She went back to bed for just a minute, but when I covered her up, she threw off the covers, saying she wished that I wouldn't put them on her (It's below freezing tonight). She got out of bed and I helped her get her robe and house shoes on, though she laughed at me as I did and said she was "already dressed for church." Then she went to sit in her chair until 1:30 a.m.

We had a good day yesterday. My mother seemed to enjoy my reading to her. And last night she enjoyed the movie we were watching and held hands with me as we watched it. Just like many times before, and how this makes me wish so much we hadn't made the decision to put her in a nursing home.

Wednesday, December 13, 1995

We were up at about 11:30 p.m. last night and sat up the remainder of the night. We had been up earlier at 8:30 p.m., with my mother seeming to be in pain and clutching her throat. I thought it was really bad indigestion and gave her something for it, and it must have helped.

When she got up at 11:30 p.m., she used the bathroom, but we had the usual potty problem then. At about 3:00 a.m. this morning, she got up and I went to the bathroom with her, but she didn't go once she got there—acted like she didn't know what to do or why she was there.

Again, we went at 4:30 a.m., and she sat down, but she couldn't use it, and got angry with me. She looked like she felt awful, and she's terribly swelled again. I thought that lying down in bed might help her, but when I asked her she said "NO!" That's ok—there's not many more of these nights, and I have a feeling that once I get some rest, I will miss even these nights of sitting up.

Thursday, December 14, 1995

My mother was up every few minutes since 7:00 p.m. last night when she went to bed until 8:00 p.m. when she went to sit in her chair. She wanted to be taken "home". Finally I got her into her robe and house shoes and took her to her chair, and she was all right. Although I was pre-pared to stay up all night again, I had a nice surprise when an hour later, around 9:00 p.m., we went back to bed. Later in the night, after she got up to use the bathroom and then went back to bed, I got hit when putting her house shoes on her. But I was lucky again. After going to the bath-room in the other side of the house, she went back to bed.

Yesterday I cried all through the day and wished so much I had not made the decision to give up on taking care of my mother. She was really sweet all day, and it just hurts so much to let her go.

Friday, December 15, 1995

We were up last night at 8:00 p.m. to sit up until 10:00 p.m. She wanted her "other bed"—her chair, because that bed she was sleeping in made her head hurt—my mother said this as she rubbed the back of her neck. It's no wonder she hurts the way she sleeps in bed. I can't get her to lie straight in bed with her head on her pillow. More and more she's curled over, with her head on the other side of the bed, and her hips up near her pillows. I won-der how they will handle something like this in the nursing home.

I've been thinking about all she won't have in the nursing home—the soft music that I play for her constantly during the daytime, which helps keep her calm. She won't have all the movies she and I watch together. She won't have the outdoors like here, the flowers, the birds, cats, and farm animals to see whenever she decides to walk outside.

She won't have me to read to her, which sometimes calms her and sometimes makes her forget whatever she thinks is going wrong. I wonder if she will let me read to her at all when I visit her in the nursing home. I wonder if our visits will be pleasant, or will she be angry and blaming me if she doesn't like it there.

There's so much to worry about, so much to fear. I don't even mind so much sitting up at night with her lately. I know I wouldn't be able to sleep anyway. I don't think I will sleep until after it's over. I'm wondering if I will be able to sleep then, with all the guilt that will surely haunt me.

Sunday, December 16, 1995

We had one more night of peaceful all-night sleep on Friday night. But we had just the opposite again last night. My mother began trying to get up soon after she went to bed. At 8:30 p.m., she came to sit in her chair, and I sat up with her for the rest of the night.

She was really nervous and easily upset all day yesterday. Around 10:30 a.m. in the morning, she wanted me to be in the kitchen cooking because she wanted all the people she saw in the room (there was only the two of us, as usual) to be fed. I was opening mail and writing Christmas cards, so I took that to the kitchen to look after lunch, which was already cooking. She followed me and insisted that I quit what I was doing and work only on the cooking. So I hurried it up and had lunch ready by 11:30 a.m. She had fallen asleep by then.

She woke up by noon and was still upset with me. She hardly ate anything, and she said she didn't want it for herself but for "those men and boys." As we left the table after lunch, she said, "They must have gone out to eat."

I'm not doing so well with Christmas this year. I have managed to send out fifteen Christmas cards and to get most of the presents wrapped, but I'm not making dozens and dozens of cookies and candies like last year. I'll make just a few, but not like previous years. I had planned not to, even if this nursing home thing wasn't coming up, because holiday preparations do seem to make my mother nervous at times.

Even though it did make her nervous last year, she did get into it and enjoyed it some. When I think back on that, I can see how much her Alzheimer's has progressed in just one year. Last year she enjoyed the Christmas tree, put icing on cookies I had baked, and even gave me money to buy presents for the family. This year she's not able to do any of that.

Friday, December 22, 1995

We've had almost a full week of my mother sleeping all night and being very pleasant, with hardly any trouble most nights. We have had just a little "potty trouble" with her not understanding that she needed to use it when she got up. Usually she would go all the way to the bathroom in the other side of the house. I was afraid that would end up in us staying up all night those nights, but it didn't. She went right back to bed, every night until last night.

Actually, she slept most of the night last night, too. She was up at 4:00 a.m. this morning, confused and worrying, saying something about "him" and "chickens." It seemed whatever I said only made her more agitated, so as usual, I let her sit in her chair, and I watched from the next room.

The way she's been so good lately really makes me regret my decision and wish there were some way to get out of it. I keep thinking back, going back through my journal and reading it, trying to figure out what was so terrible that it made me decide, once and for all, to quit taking care of her.

Sunday, December 24, 1995

We had another good night Friday night. Last night was my fault, I think, for being too sound asleep when my mother got up. If she is already out the door of the bedroom before I get awake, usually my mother is already too confused and angry because she is cold without her robe, her bare feet are on the cold floor (no carpet), and she needs to use the bathroom but doesn't know where to find it, or perhaps doesn't realize that is what she needs. I got her robe and house shoes on her, though she hit at me while I was doing it, and she was still very angry with me after sitting in her chair around 11:00 p.m. last night. When I asked if she needed anything and did she want something to drink, she just sighed, and continued staring in anger.

Something happened this afternoon that confirmed the need for my mother to be in the nursing home. The Home Health aide discovered a rash between her upper legs and lower abdomen, one like I had been taking care of with a cortisone cream at first, and then cornstarch, at her upper abdomen for many months. I had not realized this other area needed the same kind of care, because of her swelling and the way the skin is in folds there. The rash is pretty bad. The only way I can see it and take care of it is to get her to lie down on her back. With this rash, there's no wonder she's been so upset and agitated, and no wonder she couldn't sleep at night. I'm sure they will be able to take care of this problem correctly in the nursing home. I don't know if I would be able to get her to always let me do it.

There are many good reasons she will be better off. She will have skilled nursing care and continuous medical supervision. Perhaps they will discover why she is swelling so much and why she has so much indigestion. Unlike me, they have the training and skills needed for taking care of someone with Alzheimer's, and maybe it really will be what is best for her after all.

But I'm still scared—so scared about how she will handle it emotionally and for what an extreme emotional upset might do for her physically and mentally. When her environment is suddenly so different, I hope she won't, but I'm still afraid she may suffer permanent damage.

Monday December 26, 1995

We are up now at 1:00 a.m., and it is appropriate that we are, because in a few hours we will be taking my mother to the nursing home.

My mother was up early yesterday, too, though not for long. She got up for about forty-five minutes around 3:00 a.m., and then back up at 5:00 a.m. to stay.

My sister indicated yesterday that she feels the same way I do. She said she wished that we could just forget it all—just forget all about the nursing home and go on keeping our mother. But it's been arranged, paid for, and they've been holding our mother's room for several weeks now, and it's too late.

I wish we could just change our minds now and say it was a mistake and that I would keep her longer. She was so good all through Christmas Eve with everyone coming here for a little drop-in party. I did a lot less cookies and candy this year, and more healthy foods: a fruit tray, veggie tray, cheese and crackers. I still got comments like "You really know how to do a party", and "I thought you said you weren't going to do as much this year." This year having people around didn't seem to make my mother as nervous as it did last year. Once she asked me who was in the kitchen, and I said "William". She even got up and went to my brother, William, and hugged him.

Christmas Day at my sister's house went pretty well, too. My mother did get tired and started sundowning a little in the afternoon, getting really nervous and confused for a while. But I think she enjoyed most of the holiday. She even got excited yesterday morning when I was loading my car with the gifts to take to my sister's, and she was smiling and seemed to be happy most of the day.

The night has been different, though. She has been extremely nervous and confused. She's been sitting in her chair, but hasn't slept much. Just now, at 2:00 a.m., she got up, asking something that sounded like, "Did you find it?" and "I am waiting for her." She wandered around a little while, then sat back down in her chair and fell asleep again.

On Christmas Eve, we watched a home video my brother made of us all decorating the Christmas tree last year. The most amazing thing about it, other than the fact that I looked overweight last year, was that my mother was walking around by herself through the house, looking out the windows, carrying on conversations, sitting contented watching us while we decorated the tree, and smiling—always smiling. She's been so different this year, except for the surprise when she got up to go see my brother and give him a hug. Now she just sits most of the time, and though she has been smiling some this Christmas, she hasn't smiled this much in a long time.

It's almost 3:00 a.m. now. About twelve hours from now, we will be taking her to the nursing home. I've just been walking through the other side of the house to the kitchen, so I wouldn't disturb her, peeping at her from there, and then walking back through the other side with a diet cola to where I am watching from the next room. How will I be able to stand walking through this house after we have put my mother in the nursing home? Every part of it will remind me. How will I stand being here?

Being busy with all the Christmas preparations has helped me through the past few weeks and days. But on Christmas afternoon, when my niece started to leave for her trip back home to Florida, she said she would be thinking of us, and praying for us as we put her Granny in the nursing home, then I felt tears running down my face. One of my nieces had told my sister that I didn't need to go. But I do. I've got to see the nursing home, and I've got to see how my mother reacts. We're still in this together, my sister and me, and we will be through to the end, whatever happens in the nursing home, and however long she is there, until my mother passes through the final stages to the end.

It's 3:30 a.m. now. My mother is agitated. I just took her to the bathroom again. I asked if she wanted to go back to bed, thinking it might make her feel better for this day if she did, but she wouldn't. She just kept asking "Is she better?" Nothing I said would satisfy her, so I left her in her chair. As I always do I said, "I'll be in the next room if you need me", and I came to sit and watch again. My constant watching and sitting up at night will soon be over. How I wish I could be sitting in there with her, talking to her on this last night, but I can't for fear of making her more agitated when she is so confused and not understanding anything I say.

Dear Mama, on this last night together, how I wish I could just tell you how much I love you. I love you so much. What will be happening in the next few hours doesn't mean I don't love you. How I wish it didn't have to happen. How I wish...

CHAPTER 14

▼

SITTING ALONE

Alzheimer's

Sitting in your chair
in the nursing home,
you hold my hand,
but you barely respond.
You can't understand me;
I can't understand you.
Words have no meaning.
Neither do faces.
You've been on the way
here for a long time.
But did I speed it up?
In trying to care for you,
did I do more harm than good?
And then I gave up,
and now you just sit.
Mama, I'm so sorry.
Mama, I'm so afraid
that I did this to you.

Monday, January 1, 1996

We put my mother in the nursing home last Monday afternoon. This afternoon, one week later, she was taken to the hospital, and could die, with pneumonia.

Getting her to the nursing home was no problem. She was calm. She didn't even ask where we were going when my sister told her it was time to go. She went freely, smiling and content. She was still that way when we got to the nursing home, still that way when she sat in her chair there, and still seemed happy as we left, leaving her in the care of my sister-in-law, a nurse there.

She was asleep when we went to visit on Friday. And today she has pneumonia.

I can't help but feel that this is my fault. She may die tonight, and if she does, it will be my fault.

Sunday, January 7, 1996

My mother is much better, and she got out of the hospital this afternoon. We told her that she would be taken to "another hospital" this afternoon, because my sister-in-law has told her when she asked in the nursing home that she is sick and is in a place where she can be taken care of—no one has mentioned "nursing home" to her.

An ambulance delivered her back to the nursing home this afternoon and we stayed an hour or so with her. It was so hard leaving her after we had taken turns watching her around the clock, day and night, in the hospital all week. And she is so much worse than when we left her in the nursing home almost two weeks ago. She hardly has any ability to communicate at all, she is totally incontinent, and it appears that she may not even be able to walk. She has been in bed in the hospital for almost a week, and has been hooked up to all kinds of tubes much of the week—even a feeding tube in order to give her medicine and some nourishment.

She was more alert this morning than she has been all week, but she still falls asleep very quickly. It's like she can stay awake for only a few minutes at a time.

Being with her this week has made it easier in a way. It has been like a second chance to do something for her. I've sat up with her in the hospital for the last three nights. But tonight, coming back to the house was terrible, with all the memories, and feeling like I've taken so much away from her, including this house, just as she often accused me of doing. I don't know how long I can live here.

Sunday, January 14, 1996

This week has been worse for me, especially this weekend—my first one alone here since we took my mother to the nursing home.

I felt even worse after we visited her today. She was almost totally nonresponsive. She just held hands with me and moved her eyes, and she tried to whisper one word only once. Her face is badly drawn to one side—evidence of a stroke. She fell asleep while we were there.

She didn't seem to show any kind of recognition of us at all. I'm so afraid she won't be around for long. I think she's about to die, and I still feel that it is my fault. My sister and brother-in-law talked to me today about it—told me that I am not to blame. But I still feel that I am.

Tuesday, January 16, 1996

My mother is better. She has been getting angry with the aides and nurses, so there's still some life in her.

I'm doing ok, too. The weekend was awful, but keeping busy helps. I have a temporary job that started Friday. And I am invited to my sister's most every night for supper, TV, and a relaxing cup of tea, so I don't have to be alone in this house unless I want to.

I guess my mother is better off in the nursing home than with me. I was reaching my breaking point. I think she's being well taken care of. Something they are doing has even made the swelling go down, and she doesn't seem to have indigestion anymore. Could it be that they puree her food? They haven't tried to put her dentures back in. They crush her medicine, give her pureed food, and she gets a "health shake" between meals.

Still it hurts. The memories are all over this house. They are here, always right here.

[Note: The lapse in time here is due to me working, traveling to other towns, and eventually moving because of the new job. After January 16, I didn't write in my journal again until April 7.]

Sunday, April 7, 1996

My mother seemed less alert today than in recent weeks. She didn't know what to do with her birthday presents (Yesterday was her 80th birthday). We didn't wrap them but just put them in gift bags to make it easier. Still, she just pulled on the bag instead of understanding that she needed to reach inside to find her gifts. She hardly reacted at all when we pulled out her new dresses and gowns. It's like she's slowly falling into a deep sleep and losing more consciousness each day. Her periods of being aware of anything at all are getting fewer and less frequent.

For a few weeks she had seemed better. Sometimes she was even very talkative, although it was hard to understand anything she was trying to say. Two or three times when we visited, she even took walks down the hall. She has been different each time we have visited. Sometimes it seemed she was hardly awake, hardly aware of anything. Other times she has been chattering away (though she couldn't be understood), sometimes even laughing, and sometimes she seemed restless. Most of the time, though, she has seemed content. My sister-in-law says that she loves it when they take her in wheelchair to see the cloggers/line dancers that entertain in the nursing home.

I still feel guilty. I still try to escape it all. I have worked in four different towns and have now ended up in Huntsville, about as far as I can run away and still stay in Alabama, still close enough to visit her on Sundays.

Sunday, April 21, 1996

My mother was different today. She seemed more like she often was when I was taking care of her. She had that worried look on her face. She was very out of it when we arrived. I think she had just waked up and may have been dreaming. She frowned and mumbled things we couldn't understand. I held her hand and told her everything was all right. Just once I could understand what she said—something like "I just want to do what's right." I told her she was doing what was right by sitting there resting. And, because they have had trouble lately getting her to eat and to go for a bath, I told her it would be doing what was right for her to eat when they bring her food and to go get a bath when they come to get her for one. She nodded and said, "Ok", though she didn't stop frowning. She seemed to relax just a bit and her worrying decreased a little, as it usually does, when I held her hand and stroked her arm.

I brought her flowers again, as I have on every visit. There is always something blooming that I can take—an amaryllis, some other houseplant, or some cut flowers from the garden. She didn't seem to see the flowers at all this time. She didn't smile or say they were pretty as she has sometimes.

When we told her goodbye, there was no response. When I said I would bring her more flowers next time, she did say "Ok."

It felt sadder leaving today than at any time since she got out of the hospital and went back to the nursing home. For several weeks she has seemed better, but not today. I wonder if she has had more strokes.

Tuesday, April 23, 1996

My mother died early this morning, not long after midnight. She died in her sleep. The aides at the nursing home found her when they went to check on her and turn her over, as they did several times each night.

I didn't know until around 7:00 a.m. this morning, after I had already gone to work. My sister didn't want me to make the trip home from Huntsville until after daylight.

I didn't cry when I heard. But three times during the trip I started sobbing so much I could hardly drive. I feel so numb. I can't believe this has happened. Of course, we all knew it would. But not this soon. I expected many more Sunday visits to the nursing home, many more times of holding my mother's hand, many more times of taking flowers to her, perhaps a whole year or more of special days like her birthday, Mother's Day, and Christmas.

I don't know if it's harder this way with her being in the nursing home when she died, or if it would have been harder if I were still taking care of her. Either way, I guess I would still feel the guilt. The tremendous guilt I feel now is because I'm afraid I made this progress faster, and that maybe, she could have had at least another year or more if I hadn't put her in a nursing home—another year of walking around outside, seeing flowers, birds, kittens and farm animals, and special days with the family, maybe even another Christmas. I had read that there are those who die a short time after entering a nursing home, just from the shock of it and the change in environment. What I have feared so, has come to pass.

Wednesday, April 24, 1996

My mother's funeral was today. My father's nephew, the same minister who had spoke at my father's funeral eleven years ago, did my mother's service as well.

It had been hard when my dad died, but then I had made it through the funeral without crying too much. This time I couldn't. Tears kept rolling down my face all through the service.

Afterwards, people hugged me and expressed their sympathy, and it started again, rivers of tears that I couldn't stop.

I wish I could be with them, my mother and dad—the two people I loved more than anyone, and the two who loved me as only parents can. I feel so alone now. I know now what my mother longed for. "Home" doesn't really exist for me anymore, and now I understand that longing "to go home", back to the home of her childhood, to be with her Mama and Papa. I miss her so, and I don't know if the tears will ever stop for me, but she's home now.

Daddy

You were always so kind and
gentle, always by Mama's side,
and she stood by you—
took care of you till you died.
Then sorrow touched our hearts,
and Mama cried alone
till she began her journey—
her search for home.
Eleven years passed, and she
grew tired, but searched again,
till one day she was so weary,
the Father said "Come home"
and you were there to welcome her,
"Sweet darling, come on in!"

CHAPTER 15

▼

THROUGH THE TEARS

The House

My mother's house was
a place of comfort,
a place of memories,
where I grew up.
Then I put her in
a nursing home.
She didn't remember
her house anymore.
Now my mother's house is mine,
but I don't want to go there.
I try to stay away.
It's not home anymore;
My mother isn't there.
There's only memories of how I failed,
and guilt because I'm not still trying
to make her house her home.

Sunday, May 12, 1996

I went back home this weekend and spent some time with my sister. It was our first Mother's Day without our mother.

I got up early to spend an hour or so at the cemetery at my mother and dad's graves. I picked flowers to take—purple iris and red poppies. It helped to be there—crying and talking as if my mother were really there listening. I asked her to forgive me for not taking better care of her and for putting her in the nursing home.

It seems the more I cry, the more the tears flow. I wonder if I will ever stop crying.

Sunday, May 26, 1996

I was home for Memorial Day, and I went through the ritual at my mother's grave again early in this morning. I took poppies, bachelor buttons, and other flowers. There was more crying (It hasn't stopped yet), and while I was there I read a poem I've written recently, "Precious Times". The times with my mother were such precious times, and I didn't really realize just how precious until they were gone.

Everyone was together for the Memorial Day cookout, including both my nieces, and we celebrated the oldest one's thirtieth birthday. My mother's granddaughter—thirty years old.

It was nice being together, but someone was missing. In a way, just being together as we were makes it hurt more. The memories are there, and I can almost see my mother walking through the house, sitting in the porch swing, holding the puppy as she sat in the lawn chair last Fourth of July. It's like it's more than just someone I loved so much who is missing—It's like a part of me is missing and I wonder if I will ever be a whole person again.

Thursday, August 22, 1996

I have been back to my mother's grave a couple of times since May, but I haven't been back for at least a couple of months now. I have been working two jobs—trying to keep busy and to get caught up on paying bills. I still cry about my mother, but there is something that is helping me so much.

I am creating a memorial to my mother on the computer. I have a home page on the Internet in her memory, and it is growing every day as I find Alzheimer's resources links to add to it and as I share my mother's story through my journal and poetry. It seems to be helping others, because I'm already getting a lot of email from people who say it helps to make them feel they aren't alone in what they are going through.

I think my mother would like that a lot. She will live on, not only in the hearts and memories of all who knew her, but others will read about her and love her as we did. Sometimes I think of this as a gift that she gave

me—a purpose and something to do with my life after she was gone, and
a gift that I can share with others.

*Dear Mama, I still love you and miss you so, and I thank you for the gift you
gave me. Not just me, either Mama—lots of people love you and thank you.*

Precious Times

I cry a river
over times that are past,
when I held my mother's hand,
and when I made her laugh.
We walked and saw flowers
and listened to the birds;
She couldn't always understand,
but love didn't need words.
Even in the dark times,
when we were up through the night,
why didn't I see it?
Everything was right.
Why did I give up
and send her to a home?
She sat alone for a while,
and now she is gone.

Sights and Sounds

Sometimes it's a sound,
birds like we listened to,
or the music she liked to hear;
Sometimes a smell,
like flowers, or even the
shampoo she used;
Sometimes bacon frying,
or the pudding she liked.
Over and over, every day,
I think of my mother,
and tears flow.
I was so tired, but why
did I give up?
Those were the best times,
the only really important times
in all of my life.

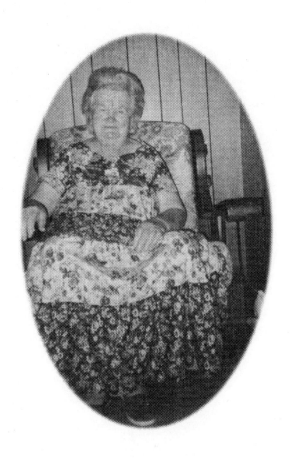

Song of Alzheimer's

My mother was so full of life
and living was a joy.
It seemed as she grew older
she just surprised me more.
I saw her as my mother;
I found her as my friend
but that was just before
the beginning of the end.
Won't somebody please
do something about Alzheimer's Disease?
Won't somebody please
do something about Alzheimer's Disease?

I took care of my mother;
I tried the best I could.
We had some really good times,
but some that weren't so good.
It seems all I can think of—
It haunts me day and night;
Re-living all the bad times
and what I didn't do right.

Won't somebody please
do something about Alzheimer's Disease?
Won't somebody please
do something about Alzheimer's Disease?

I look into the mirror;
I see my mother's face.
I reach out for something;
I see I have her hands.
I think I have her hair
now that it's turning gray.
I wonder if I'll be like her
in every way?

Won't somebody please
do something about Alzheimer's Disease?
Won't somebody please
do something about Alzheimer's Disease?

It's in most every family,
everywhere I go;
Someone's losing someone
that they love so.
These should be the best times,
not the very worst.
These are the last times;
Why do they have to hurt?

Won't somebody please
do something about Alzheimer's Disease?
Won't somebody please
do something about Alzheimer's Disease?

(note: Dorothy Womack has written music for my song above.)

What I Wish

I wish I had taken
life a little less seriously.
I wish I had taken time
to laugh with my mother.
I wish I had hugged her more,
held her hand, and said "I love you."
I wish we had enjoyed more ice cream.
I wish I had played make-believe
instead of trying to explain.
I wish I had taken time
to smell the roses,
to touch them as she did.
I wish I had felt less anger
and more love.
It was over so soon.
I wish I had realized
life would feel so empty
without her.

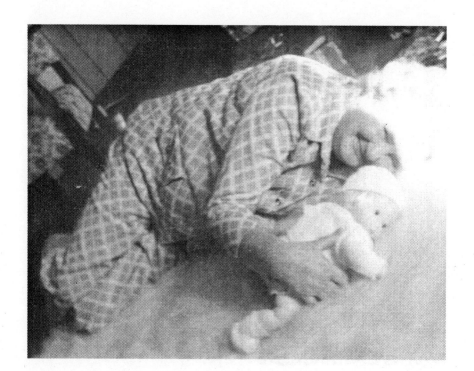

Sing to Me, Mama

Sing to me, Mama
Sing, sing a song
of high in the tree top
as we swing on the porch
of how the cradle will rock.
Sing to me, Mama
of butterflies and flowers,
kittens and pups,
of what it will be like
when I'm grown up.
Sing of rain on the rooftop,
hay in the barn,
of guardian angels
who keep us from harm.
Sing with that look and
a tear in your eye,
of a land far away,
where the soul never dies.

Now the swing hangs still
till touched by the wind,
at that house on the hill
where no one lives.
When did the bough break?
I've fallen so far
I can't go home
Home to the house,
to the swing on the porch.
Hold me tight, Mama,
Don't let me fall.
Sing to me, Mama.
Please sing again.

EPILOGUE

▼

The story didn't end with my mother's death. There is so much involved in getting through life after caregiving. Someone once told my sister that when a parent with Alzheimer's dies the grieving is already done long before they die. I can see how that could be true, but in my case, the grieving went on long after my mother's death as well. There were so many feelings of guilt, so many "what ifs" and thoughts of what might have been if I had handled some things differently.

I began a relationship with a man I worked for in the months following my mother's placement in the nursing home. We married in September of 1996, five months after my mother's death. Richard was a strong shoulder to cry on and my encourager who told me in my tear-filled months after her death that I needed to write about it. He told me I needed to get my journal out and go through it, letting my feelings out, and he provided me with the computer and Internet access that made my Web site possible. I cried for months, so much I had difficulty working. But as I worked on my Web site, collecting all the Internet links on Alzheimer's that I could find, adding my poems, my pictures, and my journal, I began to heal. The tears didn't end for a long time, but they decreased, and gradually I was able to get myself more into work, and later graduate school again as well, and eventually the numbness and pain were replaced with peace.

I had left graduate school in 1994 needing twelve more hours to com-
plete my degree. I was not able to go back in the first couple of years after
my mother's death. But in January 1998, I began taking classes again, this
time commuting a six-hour round trip once a week for classes while
working two jobs. Richard, retired by this time, was my constant support
in this effort. I was too tired, not quite well physically, and he drove me
to classes each week and sat in the library waiting for me while I was in
class and doing research. At home, when I was on the computer, he was
constantly looking over my shoulder and asking "Is that homework
you're doing?", or saying "You'd better be doing homework!" With his
encouragement, I did what had seemed impossible, and I graduated in
December 1998, with a 4.0 in my last twelve hours, which I transferred
from the University of Alabama back to Florida State University.

After I graduated we moved to another part of the state for a new posi-
tion I accepted at a university library. Miracles began happening there. In
the office next to mine was another daughter of an Alzheimer's victim. She
had lost her father to Alzheimer's, and she wanted to begin a local support
group. I helped her, and it was a wonderful success. I also had the oppor-
tunity to meet the Director of the local Alzheimer's Association Chapter
who had been so helpful to me when I was with my mother.

Another miracle happened online while I was there. Dorothy Womack
had written me previously and we began writing and chatting daily.
Dorothy had a profound influence on me spiritually, helping me find my
way back into a relationship with God that I had abandoned, helping me
realize for the first time that all of the guilt and grief could be replaced
with peace and healing. The numbness that had been with me since my
mother death left and I began to be truly happy again. Physical healing as
well as emotional resulted as well: the undifferentiated connective tissue
disease/possible lupus, possible rheumatoid arthritis I'd been diagnosed
with disappeared, and a change in medication tremendously helped the
fibromyalgia that remained. Only eight months later I again moved, to
accept a position back in the northern part of the state at a community

college where I'd worked part-time previously. This was another miracle, giving me a very exciting and fulfilling position as Technical Services (Cataloging Librarian)/Reference Librarian and Webmaster at the library. As the library's Webmaster, I am using the skills I had developed while working on *A Year to Remember*, my Web site in memory of my mother.

Dorothy Womack wrote a poem for me that I'd like to share here:

Most of All
by Dorothy Womack

I wish I could have told you
All the things I couldn't say—
Of how important you are to me
It's always been that way.
You were the brunt of my abuse
And blamed yourself——The more
I argued and antagonized
Added to the load you bore.
You must believe I didn't mean
The cruel words I said—
Nor would I ever willfully
Punish you, or inflict dread.
Deep down, you knew, I'd lost control
This was not really 'me'—
You longed to see me 'come alive'
Yet, this was not meant to be.
I've followed you, as you've progressed
To finally gain your dreams—
All your hard work and sacrifice
God's blessed-Indeed, it seems.

We've both moved on to greater sights
Each, to prosper, where we're called—
Remember-I'm within your heart
And I love you—Most of all....

Copyright © 1998 Dorothy Womack
Used with permission of the author.

Yes, there is life after caregiving. And there is healing for all the tormented guilt and grief-filled thoughts. There is forgiveness for anything we did that should have been done differently. There is hope, so much hope, for being reunited with the one we love someday, hope for a better world until then, hope for a cure for Alzheimer's, or at least better medications to control it and/or prevent or delay it.

My greatest hope is that you will feel a little more informed and a little less alone because I've shared my story. Because I've lived through this, you can too. You have the strength and courage that you need, and you can cherish each moment that remains with your Alzheimer's patient. God bless you!

I'll Remember

Last year it hurt
to hear the birds sing;
and to see the first flowers
that marked the coming of Spring;
To taste something new
my mother would have liked,
to see a sunset,
or a full moon at night.
This year it doesn't
hurt quite so bad,
and I feel so grateful
for the year that I had.
Through good times and bad times
the love that we shared
has colored my world
and helped to prepare
for telling our story—
The gift that she gave.
I'll remember my mother
through all of my days.

Singing Trees

It must have been twice
that year. In the Spring and in the
fall. The trees in the back yard would
come alive, covered in birds. I would
say to my mother: "Look, there's the
singing trees!" She would point to
the bird feeders on the windows,
and talk to the birds, even if there
were none there. Like she talked
to the flowers when we took our walks.
Such a delightful world it was at times,
talking to flowers and bird feeders,
and listening to singing trees.

Out That Door

Out that door we watched snow fall
on pansies in the winter,
and sometimes on daffodils and even
tulips in the spring.
We watched deer prance
through the yard,
and wild turkeys gobble
down the hill.
We watched squirrels climbing
the clothesline, or coming
to visit bird feeders on the window.
We watched birds come and go, telling
the seasons by their arrival
and departure.

Out that door we walked most
every day, to get a closer look,
at wildlife and flowers
and to walk with Pansy, the cat.
My mother held my hand,
and I got to know her more
each day, as parts of her
past came to life.
Though there might be confusion
and terror in the night,
out that door we found peace,
a refuge from the storm.

Little Girl Again

She walked with me to see the flowers
And the kittens near the barn.
She talked to them, "Kitty, kitty"
as I held her by the arm.

She didn't eat much lunch
but rather wanted sweets.
She got upset when I scolded,
and pouted until she went to sleep.

She was delighted again
when snack time came,
And she loved sitting all afternoon
in the front porch swing.

Again she didn't eat much
At the evening meal
And she grew so very sleepy
She could hardly sit still.

I hugged her and tucked her in,
And told her goodnight.
But not much later she awoke,
Crying out in fright.

"Where are my momma and poppa?
Why did they leave me here?"
She sobbed "I want to go home"
as I wiped her tears.

Trapped in the body of
A woman of seventy-nine—
I always wanted a little girl.
My mother now is mine.

Mama's Quilts

My mother could make magic
from little scraps of fabric.
Forgotten dresses of long ago
became beautiful quilts
that kept memories alive
and warmed us at night.
There didn't have to be
a pattern, just love
in every stitch.
That love lives, though
she has gone, and
her quilts are worn.
In every fabric of memory,
every story, every poem.
I'll put together pieces
of our lives, like a
quilt to keep us warm.

Heroes

For all of you, my caregiving heroes—
I did it for only a year, but many of you
have for years. God bless you, my heroes!

The caregivers are my heroes
who live with grief each day
as they are watching loved ones
slowly fade away.
They put their own lives on hold
to be with a parent or a spouse
They give and give all they can
until they are given out.

They get tired and discouraged,
sometimes angry and grief-filled,
but yet they try their best
and to despair do not yield.
God bless my heroes, the caregivers,
bless them in every way.
Give them peace each night
and courage for each new day

ABOUT THE AUTHOR

Brenda Parris Sibley is author/Webmaster of the award-winning Web site, *A Year to Remember…with My Mother and Alzheimer's Disease,* which is located at http://www.zarcrom.com/users/yeartorem/. She also is list owner of *Top Alzheimer's/Caregiving Sites* at http://new.topsitelists.com/bestsites/bpsibley, a mailing list reviewing these sites at http://groups.yahoo.com/group/TopADCaregivingSites, and maintains the *Top Alzheimer's/Caregiving Sites Community* at iUniverse: http://communities.iuniverse.com/bin/circle.asp?circleid=6622. Brenda was caregiver from August 1994 through December 1995 for her mother who had Alzheimer's. Her mother passed away on April 23, 1996 after being in a nursing home for four months. Brenda is a librarian at a community college and lives with her husband Richard in Decatur, Alabama. She may be contacted at bpsibley@mindspring.com.

BIBLIOGRAPHY

▼

There are so many books I could list here as suggested reading, but I am listing only the ones I've read and/or have noticed are especially highly recommended. A more extensive bibliography and filmography can be found on my Web site at http://www.zarcrom.com/users/yeartorem/bibliographies.html.

About Alzheimer's and Caregiving

Bridges, Barbara J. *Therapeutic Caregiving: a Practical Guide for Caregivers of Persons with Alzheimer's and Other Dementia Causing Diseases*. Mill Creek, WA: BJB Pub., 1996.

Coughlan, Patricia Brown. *Facing Alzheimer's: Family Caregivers Speak*. New York: Ballantine Books, 1993.

Davies, Helen P. and Michael P. Jensen. *Alzheimer's: the Answers You Need*. Forest Knolls, CA: Elder Books, 1998.

Davidson, Frena Gray. *Alzheimer's FAQ: frequently asked questions, making sense of the journey*. Los Angeles: Lowell House, 1997.

Davidson, Frena Gray. *The Alzheimer's Sourcebook for Caregivers*. Los Angeles: Lowell House, 1993.

Dunn, Hank. *Hard Choices for Loving People: CPR, Artificial Feeding, Comfort Measures Only and the Elderly Patient.* 3rd ed., Herndon, VA: A & A Publishers (P.O. Box 1098, Herndon, VA 20172-1098), 1994.

Granet, Roger, M.D. & Eileen Fallon. *Is It Alzheimer's?: What To Do When Loved Ones Can't Remember What They Should.* New York: Avon, 1998.

Haisman, Pam. *Alzheimer's Disease: Caregiver's Speak Out.* Chippendale House Publishers, 1998.

Hall, Geri. *As Memory Fades—The Caregivers Challenge Begins: Understanding and Coping with Problem Behaviors Related to Memory Loss: A Learning Guide.* Scottsdale, AZ (13400 E. Shea Boulevard, Scottsdale, AZ 85259): Mayo Clinic, [1999?].

Hay, Jennifer. *Alzheimer's & Dementia: questions you have—answers you need.* Allentown, Pa.: People's Medical Society, 1996.

Hendershott, Anne. *The Reluctant Caregivers: Learning to Care for a Loved One with Alzheimer's Disease.* Westport, CT: Bergin & Garvey, 2000.

Hodgson, Harriet W. *Alzheimer's: Finding the Words.* Minneapolis, MN: Chronimed Pub., 1995.

Keck, David. *Forgetting whose we are: Alzheimer's Disease and the Love of God.* Nashville: Abingdon Press, 1996.

Mace, Nancy L. & Peter V. Rabins. *The 36-Hour Day.* 3rd ed., Baltimore: Johns Hopkins Univ, 1999.

McKim, Donald K. *God Never Forgets: Faith, Hope, and Alzheimer's Disease.* Westminister/John Knox, 1997.

McLeod, Beth Witrogen. *Caregiving: The Spiritual Journey of Love, Loss, and Renewal.* New York: John Wiley & Sons, 1999.

Naughtin, Gerry and Terry Laidler. *When I Grow Too Old to Dream: Coping with Alzheimer's Disease.* North Blackburn, Australia: Collins Dove, 1991.

Ostuni, Elizabeth. *Getting Through: Communicating When Someone You Care for Has Alzheimer's Disease.* Vero Beach, FL: Speech Bin, 1991.

Pollen, Daniel A. *Hannah's Heirs: The Quest for the Genetic Origins of Alzheimer's Disease.* Oxford Univ. Press, 1996. Post, Stephen G. The Moral Challenge of Alzheimer's Disease, 1997

Strecker, Tereas R. *Alzheimer's: Making Sense of Suffering.* Huntington House, 1997

Warner, Mark. *The Complete Guide to Alzheimer's-Proofing Your Home.* West Lafayette, IN: Purdue University Press, 1998.

Biographies and Personal Stories

Anifantaskis, Harry. *The Diminished Mind: The Jean Tyler Story.* Blue Ridge Summit, PA: Tab Books, 1991.

Bayley, John. *Elegy for Iris.* New York: St. Martin's Press, 1999.

Bristow, Lois. *Will I be next? the terror of living with familial Alzheimer's Disease: Bea Gorman's life story.* Acampo, CA: Hope Warrne Press, 1996.

Caldwell, Marianne. *Gone without a Trace.* Forest Knolls, CA: Elder Books, 1995.

Cassel, Franklin K. *Flowers for Peggy.* Lancaster, PA. (Brethren Village, P.O. Box 5093): F. Cassel, 1997.

Combs, Linda. *A Long Goodbye.* Winston Salem, NC: Combs Publishing.

Danna, Jo. *When Alzheimer's Hits Home.* Briarwood, NY: Palomino Press, 1995.

Davis, Patti. *A Long Goodbye.* New York: Alfred A. Knopf, 1997.

Davis, Robert and Betty. *My Journey into Alzheimer's Disease.* Wheaton, IL: Tyndale House Pub., 1969.

Henderson, Cary Smith. *Partial view: an Alzheimer's Journal.* Dallas, TX: Southern Methodist University Press, 1998.

McGowin, Diana Friel. *Living in the Labyrinth: a Personal Journey through the Maze of Alzheimer's.* New York: Delacorte Press, 1993. Large print ed.: Thorndike, ME: Thorndike Press, c1993

Murphy, Beverly Bigtree. *He Used to Be Somebody: a journey into Alzheimer's Disease through the eyes of a caregiver*. Boulder, Colo.: Gibbs Associates, c1995.

Rose, Larry. *Show Me the Way to Go Home*. Forest Knolls, CA: Elder Books, 1996.

Shanks, Lela Knox. *Your Name is Hughes Hannibal Shanks: a Caregiver's Guide to Alzheimer's*. Lincoln: University of Nebraska Press, 1996.

Spohr, Betty Baker. *To Hold a Falling Star*. Seattle, WA: Longmeadow Press, 1990.

Starkman, Elain Marcus. *Learning to Sit in Silence*. Watsonville, CA: Papier-Mache Press, 1993.

Walsh, Mary B. *One Family's Journey through Alzheimer's*. Wheaton, Ill.: Tyndale House, 2000.

Zabbia, Kim Howes. *Painted diaries: a mother and daughter's experience through Alzheimer's*. Minneapolis: Fairview Press, 1996.

Alzheimer's in Poetry

Cherry, Kelly. "Alzheimer's" In *Death and Transfiguration*. Louisiana State University Press, 1997.

Ham, Jerry. *This Stranger in Our House*. Spokane, WA: The Inland Northwest Chapter of the Alzheimer's Association (720 W. Boone Ave., Suite 101, Spokane, WA 99201), 1999.

MacDonald, Hugh. *Looking for Mother*. Windsor, Canada: Black Moss Press, 1995.

Children's Books

Bahr, Mary. *The Memory Box*. Morton Grove, IL: A Whitman, 1992.

Bauer, Marion Dan. *An early winter*. New York: Clarion Books, 1999.

Casey, Barbara. *Grandma Jock & Christabelle*. Nashville, TN: J.C. Winston Pub. Co., 1995.

Graber, Richard. *Doc*. New York: Harper & Row, 1986.

Gruenewald, Nancy. *Grandpa Forgot My Name*. Illustrated by Bruce Loeschen. Austin, MN: Newborn Books, c1997.

Guthrie, Donna. *Grandpa Doesn't Know It's Me*. New York: Human Sciences Press, 1986.

Karkowsky, Nancy Faye. *Grandma's Soup*. Rockville, MD: Kar-Ban Copies, 1989.

Kelley, Barbara. *Harpo's horrible secret*. Prairie Grove, Ark.: Ozark Pub., 1996.

Kibbey, Marsha. *My Grammy*. Minneapolis, MN: Carolrhoda Books, 1988.

Kroll, Virginia L. *Fireflies, Peach Pies, & Lullabies*. New York: Simon & Schuster, 1995.

Mackall, Dandi Daley. *Horse Whispers in the Air*. St. Louis, MO: Concordia Pub. House, 2000

Sanford, Doris. *Maria's Grandma Gets Mixed Up*. Portland, OR: Multnomah, 1989.

Shawyer, Margaret. *What's wrong with Grandma?: a Family Experience with Alzheimer's*. Amherst, NY: Prometheus Books, 1996.

Shecter, Ben. *Great-Uncle Alfred Forgets*. New York: Harper Collins, 1996.

Smith, Doris Buchanan. *Remember the Red-Shouldered Hawk*. New York: G. P. Putnam's Sons, 1994.

Whitelaw, Nancy. *A Beautiful Pearl*. Morton Grove, Ill.: A. Whitman, 1991.

Williams, Carol Lynch. *If I Forget, You Remember*. New York: Delacorte Press, 1998.

Web Sites

Again, I make no attempt to include all Web sites on Alzheimer's and care-giving, for there are too many. A whole book could be written on these and other related Internet sites.

AlzBrainOrg-http://www.alzbrain.org/index.html

Alzheimer's Association-http://www.alz.org/

Alzheimer's Disease at
About.com–http://alzheimers.about.com/health/alzheimers

Alzheimer's Disease International–http://www.alz.co.uk

Alzheimer's Page at Washington University, St. Louis-
http://www.adrc.wustl.edu/alzheimer/

Alzheimer Europe-http://www.alzheimer-europe.org/

Alzheimer's Society of Canada–http://www.alzheimer.ca/

CANDID-http://candid.ion.ucl.ac.uk/candid/

Caregiver.com-http://www.caregiver.com/

Caregiver's Army-http://www.caregiversarmy.org/

Caregiver's SEAD-http://neuro-oas.mgh.harvard.edu/sea/

Caregiving Online-http://www.caregiving.com/

ElderCare Online-http://www.ec-online.net/

Empowering Caregivers-http://www.care-givers.com/

Partners Program of Excellence in Alzheimer's and Other Neurodegenerative
Diseases-http://neuro-oas.mgh.harvard.edu/alzheimers/

The Ribbon-http://www.theribbon.com/index.html

Personal Home Pages

Alzheimer's Outreach, by Marsha Penington-
http://www.zarcrom.com/users/alzheimers/index1.html

Alzwell, by Susan Grossman-http://www.webcom.com/~susan/welcome.html

Caregiver's Haven, by Nancy Walker-
http://www.nhisgarden.com/caregivers/entrance.html

Hoffmann Family Homepage, by Bob Hoffman-
http://www.bhoffcomp.com/coping

Kate's Place, by Kate Murphy-http://home.att.net/~katesdrm/

The Long Goodbye, by Penny Klein-
http://www.geocities.com/Wellesley/Garden/5337/index.html

Passage into Paradise, by Dorothy Womack-
http://www.geocities.com/womack47/passage.html

Poems, Prayers, and Promises, by Brenda Race-
http://www.geocities.com/brace03/Mom.html

Undying Love, by Patrick Davison-
http://denver.rockymountainnews.com/undyinglove

Home Pages by Patients

Diana McGowin's Home Page-
http://hometown.aol.com/lilauthor1/index.html

Jan/Mina's Home Page-http://www.ycsi.net/users/laura/janmina.html

Laura's Home Page, by Laura Smith-http://www.ycsi.net/users/laura/

Mary's Place, by Mary Lockhart-
http://www.nhisgarden.com/caregivers/entrance.html

My Journey, by Chip Gerber-
http://www.zarcrom.com/users/alzheimers/chip.html

Simple Pleasures, by Peter Smith-
http://www.zarcrom.com/users/alzheimers/peter1.html

Thru His Eyes, by Tim Brennan-
http://www.nhisgarden.com/his_eyes/entrance.html